studysync®

Reading & Writing Companion

Making Your Mark

What's your story?

:: studysync®

studysync.com

ISBN 978-1-94-469577-4

1 2 3 4 5 6 QVS 24 23 22 21 20 19

A

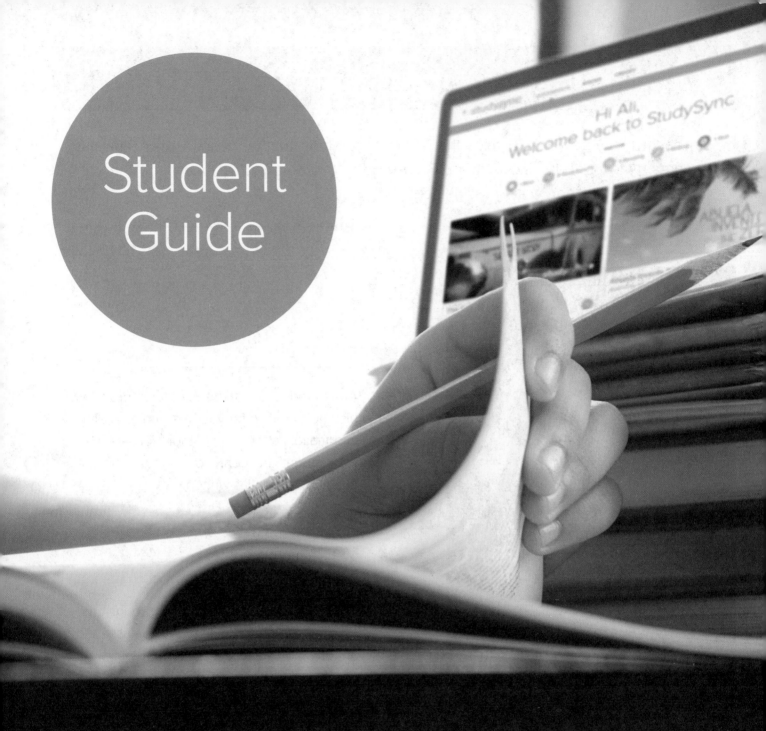

Student Guide

Getting Started

Welcome to the StudySync Reading & Writing Companion! In this book, you will find a collection of readings based on the theme of the unit you are studying. As you work through the readings, you will be asked to answer questions and perform a variety of tasks designed to help you closely analyze and understand each text selection. Read on for an explanation of each

Close Reading and Writing Routine

In each unit, you will read texts that share a common theme, despite their different genres, time periods, and authors. Each reading encourages a closer look through questions and a short writing assignment.

Eleven

FICTION
Sandra Cisneros
1991

Introduction

studysync

S andra Cisneros (b. 1954) is a renowned Chicana writer whose poems, novels, and short stories explore the complicated struggle of finding one's own identity. Cisneros is best known for her novel *The House on Mango Street* and the collection *Woman Hollering Creek and Other Stories*. "Eleven" is from the latter, the story of a girl named Rachel who experiences growing pains on her eleventh birthday. When her teacher insists that an ugly red sweater belongs to Rachel, the eleven-year-old has exceptional thoughts but can't share them. Even so, it's evident that the protagonist of Sandra Cisneros's short story has insight beyond her years.

Eleven

"You open your eyes and everything's just like yesterday, only it's today. And you don't feel eleven at all."

1 What they don't understand about birthdays and what they never tell you is that when you're eleven, you're also ten, and nine, and eight, and seven, and six, and five, and four, and three, and two, and one. And when you wake up on your eleventh birthday you expect to feel eleven, but you don't. You open your eyes and everything's just like yesterday, only it's today. And you don't feel eleven at all. You feel like you're still ten. And you are—underneath the year that makes you eleven.

2 Like some days you might say something stupid, and that's the part of you that's still ten. Or maybe some days you might need to sit on your mama's lap because you're scared, and that's the part of you that's five. And maybe one day when you're all grown up maybe you will need to cry like if you're three, and that's okay. That's what I tell Mama when she's sad and needs to cry. Maybe she's feeling three.

3 Because the way you grow old is kind of like an onion or like the rings inside a tree trunk or like my little wooden dolls that fit one inside the other, each year inside the next one. That's how being eleven years old is.

4 You don't feel eleven. Not right away. It takes a few days, weeks even, sometimes even months before you say Eleven when they ask you. And you don't feel smart eleven, not until you're almost twelve. That's the way it is.

5 Only today I wish I didn't have only eleven years rattling inside me like pennies in a tin Band-Aid box. Today I wish I was one hundred and two instead of eleven because if I was one hundred and two I'd have known what to say when Mrs. Price put the red sweater on my desk. I would've known how to tell her it wasn't mine instead of just sitting there with that look on my face and nothing coming out of my mouth.

6 "Whose is this?" Mrs. Price says, and she holds the red sweater up in the air for all the class to see. "Whose? It's been sitting in the coatroom for a month."

 Skill: Figurative Language

The narrator uses similes when she compares aging to everyday things. When I picture onions, tree trunks, and wooden dolls, I notice they all have layers. She must mean that when you get older, you keep getting more layers.

① Introduction

An Introduction to each text provides historical context for your reading as well as information about the author. You will also learn about the genre of the text and the year in which it was written.

② Notes

Many times, while working through the activities after each text, you will be asked to **annotate** or **make annotations** about what you are reading. This means that you should highlight or underline words in the text and use the "Notes" column to make comments or jot down any questions you have. You may also want to note any unfamiliar vocabulary words here.

You will also see sample student annotations to go along with the Skill lesson for that text.

 Reading & Writing Companion

First Read

During your first reading of each selection, you should just try to get a general idea of the content and message of the reading. Don't worry if there are parts you don't understand or words that are unfamiliar to you. You'll have an opportunity later to dive deeper into the text.

Think Questions

These questions will ask you to start thinking critically about the text, asking specific questions about its purpose, and making connections to your prior knowledge and reading experiences. To answer these questions, you should go back to the text and draw upon specific evidence to support your responses. You will also begin to explore some of the more challenging vocabulary words in the selection.

Skills

Each Skill includes two parts: Checklist and Your Turn. In the Checklist, you will learn the process for analyzing the text. The model student annotations in the text provide examples of how you might make your own notes following the instructions in the Checklist. In the Your Turn, you will use those same instructions to practice the skill.

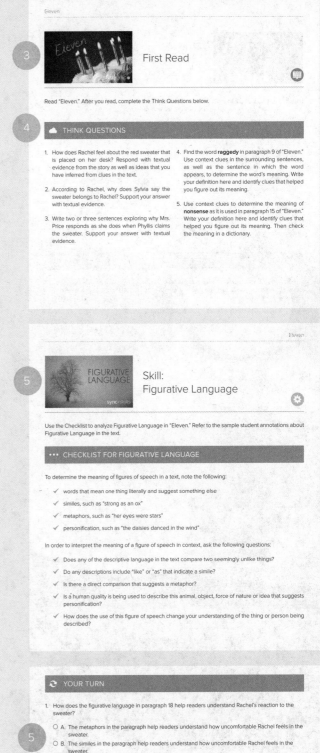

Eleven

First Read

Read "Eleven." After you read, complete the Think Questions below.

THINK QUESTIONS

1. How does Rachel feel about the red sweater that is placed on her desk? Respond with textual evidence from the story as well as ideas that you have inferred from clues in the text.

2. According to Rachel, why does Sylvia say the sweater belongs to Rachel? Support your answer with textual evidence.

3. Write two or three sentences exploring why Mrs. Price responds as she does when Phyllis claims the sweater. Support your answer with textual evidence.

4. Find the word **raggedy** in paragraph 9 of "Eleven." Use context clues in the surrounding sentences, as well as the sentence in which the word appears, to determine the word's meaning. Write your definition here and identify clues that helped you figure out its meaning.

5. Use context clues to determine the meaning of **nonsense** as it is used in paragraph 15 of "Eleven." Write your definition here and identify clues that helped you figure out its meaning. Then check the meaning in a dictionary.

Eleven

Skill: Figurative Language

Use the Checklist to analyze Figurative Language in "Eleven." Refer to the sample student annotations about Figurative Language in the text.

CHECKLIST FOR FIGURATIVE LANGUAGE

To determine the meaning of figures of speech in a text, note the following:

- ✓ words that mean one thing literally and suggest something else
- ✓ similes, such as "strong as an ox"
- ✓ metaphors, such as "her eyes were stars"
- ✓ personification, such as "the daisies danced in the wind"

In order to interpret the meaning of a figure of speech in context, ask the following questions:

- ✓ Does any of the descriptive language in the text compare two seemingly unlike things?
- ✓ Do any descriptions include "like" or "as" that indicate a simile?
- ✓ Is there a direct comparison that suggests a metaphor?
- ✓ Is a human quality being used to describe this animal, object, force of nature or idea that suggests personification?
- ✓ How does the use of this figure of speech change your understanding of the thing or person being described?

YOUR TURN

1. How does the figurative language in paragraph 18 help readers understand Rachel's reaction to the sweater?

   ○ A. The metaphors in the paragraph help readers understand how uncomfortable Rachel feels in the sweater.
   ○ B. The similes in the paragraph help readers understand how uncomfortable Rachel feels in the sweater.
   ○ C. The metaphors in the paragraph make it clear to readers that Rachel is overreacting about the sweater.
   ○ D. The similes in the paragraph make it clear to readers that Rachel is overreacting about the sweater.

2. How does the figurative language in paragraph 19 help readers visualize Rachel's behavior?

   ○ A. The mention of "little animal noises" tells readers that Rachel is acting more like an animal than a human.
   ○ B. The metaphor of "clown-sweater arms" shows that Rachel is able to see the humorous side in her experience.
   ○ C. The similes about her body shaking "like when you have the hiccups" and her head hurting "like when you drink milk too fast" connect to unpleasant experiences most readers have had.
   ○ D. The statement that "there aren't any more tears left in [her] eyes" suggests that Rachel is starting to calm down.

Close Read

6

Reread "Eleven." As you reread, complete the Skills Focus questions below. Then use your answers and annotations from the questions to help you complete the Write activity.

◎ SKILLS FOCUS

1. Identify examples of figurative language and explain the purpose they achieve in the story.

2. Explain what you can infer about the narrator's feelings about the sweater based on her descriptions, actions, and reactions.

3. The narrator uses figurative language, including similes and metaphors, to describe aging. Identify these in the text. Explain what type of figurative language each one is an example of and what each piece of figurative language means.

4. Explain what the author implies about what the narrator really wants when she says, "today I wish I was one hundred and two."

5. Getting older can be tough. Identify and explain the textual evidence in the story that supports this statement.

✎ WRITE

7

LITERARY ANALYSIS: How does the author's use of figurative language help readers understand the feelings that the narrator is expressing? Write a response of at least 200 words. Support your writing with evidence from the text.

Reading & Writing Companion **11**

Lost Island

FICTION

8

Introduction

Marina wakes up alone, thirsty, and hungry on a deserted island. How did she get here, and why is her head throbbing? As she slowly recalls a large wave smashing into Uncle Merlin's fishing boat, Marina takes her first steps towards survival.

📷 VOCABULARY

8

damp
wet

capsized
tipped over in the water

intense
very strong

rescuer
someone who saves a person from harm or danger

---

6 ## Close Read & Skills Focus

After you have completed the First Read, you will be asked to go back and read the text more closely and critically. Before you begin your Close Read, you should read through the Skills Focus to get an idea of the concepts you will want to focus on during your second reading. You should work through the Skills Focus by making annotations, highlighting important concepts, and writing notes or questions in the "Notes" column. Depending on instructions from your teacher, you may need to respond online or use a separate piece of paper to start expanding on your thoughts and ideas.

7 ## Write

Your study of each selection will end with a writing assignment. For this assignment, you should use your notes, annotations, personal ideas, and answers to both the Think and Skills Focus. Be sure to read the prompt carefully and address each part of it in your writing.

8 ## English Language Learner

The English Language Learner texts focus on improving language proficiency. You will practice learning strategies and skills in individual and group activities to become better readers, writers, and speakers.

Extended Writing Project

This is your opportunity to use genre characteristics and craft to compose meaningful, longer written works exploring the theme of each unit. You will draw information from your readings, research, and own life experiences to complete the assignment.

1 Writing Project

After you have read all of the unit text selections, you will move on to a writing project. Each project will guide you through the process of writing your essay. Student models will provide guidance and help you organize your thoughts. One unit ends with an **Extended Oral Project** which will give you an opportunity to develop your oral language and communication skills.

2 Writing Process Steps

There are four steps in the writing process: Plan, Draft, Revise, and Edit and Publish. During each step, you will form and shape your writing project, and each lesson's peer review will give you the chance to receive feedback from your peers and teacher.

3 Writing Skills

Each Skill lesson focuses on a specific strategy or technique that you will use during your writing project. Each lesson presents a process for applying the skill to your own work and gives you the opportunity to practice it to improve your writing.

Making Your Mark

What's your story?

Genre Focus: DRAMA

Texts

 Comparing Within and Across Genres

Extended Oral Project: Oral Presentation

English Language Learner Resources

What's your story?

MELBA PATTILLO BEALS

Melba Pattillo Beals (b. 1941) was twelve years old when segregation in public schools was ruled unconstitutional by the Supreme Court in *Brown v. Board of Education* in 1954. Three years later, Beals would go down in history as among the first to integrate Little Rock Central High School as part of the Little Rock Nine. For weeks, Beals made headline news all around the country, and as she navigated a relationship with the media, she decided to pursue a career as a journalist and news reporter.

LANGSTON HUGHES

The final line of the poem "I, Too," by Langston Hughes (1902 – 1967) is chiseled in the stone wall of the National Museum of African American History and Culture in Washington, DC: "I, too, am America." Hughes first wrote these words in 1926 as a young poet at the forefront of the Harlem Renaissance in New York. Through the lasting impact of his poems, Hughes continues to edify and give voice to the African American experience in the United States.

WILLIAM GIBSON

William Gibson (1914–2008) was a playwright who grew up in the Bronx. He prepared to write for the theater by first working as an actor, stage manager, and a prop person for the Topeka Civic Theater in Kansas. When his writing career took off in the 1950s, he garnered worldwide recognition for two plays, *The Miracle Worker* (1957) and *Two for the Seesaw* (1958). Both plays featured women at their center, and, like many of Gibson's scripts, dealt with historical eras and characters.

SHIRLEY JACKSON

When American writer Shirley Jackson (1916–1965) broke onto the literary scene in 1948 with the publication of her short story, "The Lottery," readers of *The New Yorker* sent more letters than the magazine had ever received in response to a piece. The gruesome ritual of a New England community that Jackson described had been mistaken for truth. Later in Jackson's career, she turned toward stories that drew on her experience as a mother, often crafting stories about ordinary domestic life.

HELEN KELLER

Helen Keller (1880–1968) spent most of her life advocating for social and political issues, and co-founded the American Civil Liberties Union in 1920. Her autobiography, *The Story of My Life* (1903), tells of the illness that took Keller's sight and hearing at nineteen months old, and of the remarkable triumphs over adversity that would make her the first deaf-blind individual to receive a bachelor of arts degree.

PIRI THOMAS

Born to a Puerto Rican mother and Cuban father, Piri Thomas (1928–2011) grew up in Spanish Harlem in New York City. In his best-selling memoir *Down These Mean Streets* (1967), Thomas explored how the pressures of a childhood infused with racism and gang violence drew him into drug addiction, crime, and eventually prison. After serving his seven-year sentence, Thomas channeled his life experience toward helping at-risk youth through stories, lectures, and workshops.

DIANA CHANG

Diana Chang (b. 1934) is an author from New York City. She spent most of her childhood in China, and returned with her family to the United States to attend college and begin her career as a literary editor, and an author of fiction and poetry. Chang's first novel, *The Frontiers of Love* (1994), is considered the first major Chinese American literary work, and, like much of her writing, explores and challenges cross-cultural identity.

FAN KISSEN

Fan Kissen (1904–1978) was an American author of biographies of historical figures such as Sacagawea, Thomas Jefferson, Benjamin Franklin, and Clara Barton. In the 1940s and 1950s, Kissen had a radio series called *Tales from the Four Winds*, where she transformed folk tales from around the world into "plays for the loudspeaker," which were broadcast directly into classrooms at the time. Before becoming an author, Kissen taught elementary school in her home in New York City.

THANHHA LAI

Poet and novelist Thanhha Lai (b. 1965) writes memorably about both of her homes—Vietnam and the United States. Lai fled Saigon in 1975 to live in Alabama and eventually earn college and graduate degrees in Texas and New York. She dedicated her first book to the millions of refugees in the world because she believes that stories of the displaced are "essential to understanding who we are, how we arrived in our home, and what responsibilities we have toward those still searching for a home."

LENSEY NAMIOKA

Lensey Namioka (b. 1929) cites adventure stories as her first love. At the age of nine, she moved with her family from China to the United States and initially excelled in math, because numerals were the same in the English classroom as in her native country. She even became a professor of mathematics, before steering her career back to the creation of fiction. Namioka is best known for the Zenta and Matsuzo Samurai series, which follows the adventures of two 16th-century samurai warriors.

Warriors Don't Cry

INFORMATIONAL TEXT
Melba Pattillo Beals
1994

Introduction

In 1954, the Supreme Court decision *Brown vs. the Board of Education* of Topeka, Kansas declared that segregation was unconstitutional and schools must be integrated. To thwart the efforts of the Arkansas governor to keep the first nine black students, including Melba Pattillo Beals, out of Central High School, President Eisenhower sent federal troops to Little Rock to make sure the students got in safely. In this excerpt from her memoir, *Warriors Don't Cry*, Beals describes how the soldiers escorted them through the crowds into the school.

"Groups of soldiers on guard were lined at intervals several feet apart."

1   The next morning, Wednesday, September 25, at 8 A.M., as we turned the corner near the Bateses' home, I saw them, about fifty uniformed soldiers of the 101st. Some stood still with their rifles at their sides, while others manned the jeeps parked at the curb. Still other troops walked about holding walkie-talkies to their ears. As I drew nearer to them I was fascinated by their well-shined boots. Grandma had always said that well-kept shoes were the mark of a disciplined individual. Their guns were also glistening as though they had been polished, and the creases were sharp in the pant legs of their uniforms.

2   I had heard all those newsmen say "Screaming Eagle Division of the 101st," but those were just words. I was seeing human beings, flesh-and-blood men with eyes that looked back at me. They resembled the men I'd seen in army pictures on TV and on the movie screen. Their faces were white, their expressions blank.

3   There were lots of people of both races standing around, talking to one another in whispers. I recognized some of the ministers from our churches. Several of them nodded or smiled at me. I was a little concerned because many people, even those who knew me well, were staring as though I were different from them.

4   Thelma and Minnijean stood together inspecting the soldiers close up while the other students milled about. I wondered what we were waiting for. I was told there was an assembly at Central with the military briefing the students.

5   Reporters hung from trees, perched on fences, stood on cars and darted about with their usual urgency. Cameras were flashing on all sides. There was an **eerie** hush over the crowd, not unlike the way I'd seen folks behave outside the home of the deceased just before a funeral.

6   There were tears in Mother's eyes as she whispered good-bye. "Make this day the best you can," she said.

7   "Let's bow our heads for a word of prayer." One of our ministers stepped from among the others and began to say some comforting words. I noticed tears

NOTES

Skill:
Informational
Text Structure

The signal words "the next morning" as well as the day, date, and time are all clues that the author is presenting events in chronological order. This shows me that this is the beginning of a real-life account being told in the text.

Skill:
Informational
Text Structure

The author is using a different text structure here that continues to develop the author's story. She contrasts the experience of hearing about the Screaming Eagle Division and actually seeing them in the flesh. Then she compares them with the men she has seen on TV.

were streaming down the faces of many of the adults. I wondered why they were crying and just at that moment when I had more hope of staying alive and keeping safe than I had since the **integration** began.

8   "Protect those youngsters and bring them home. Flood the Holy Spirit into the hearts and minds of those who would attack our children."

9   "Yes, Lord," several voices echoed.

10 One of the soldiers stepped forward and beckoned the driver of a station wagon to move it closer to the driveway. Two jeeps moved forward, one in front of the station wagon, one behind. Guns were mounted on the hoods of the jeeps.

11 We were already a half hour late for school when we heard the order "Move out" and the leader motioned us to get into the station wagon. As we collected ourselves and walked toward the caravan, many of the adults were crying openly. When I turned to wave to Mother Lois, I saw tears streaming down her cheeks. I couldn't go back to comfort her.

Skill:
Word Patterns and Relationships

I haven't seen the word breakneck used before, but it must be an adjective because it describes the speed of the soldiers.

12 Sarge, our driver, was friendly and pleasant. He had a Southern accent, different from ours, different even from the one Arkansas whites had. We rolled away from the curb lined with people waving at us. Mama looked even more **distraught**. I remembered I hadn't kissed her good-bye.

13 Our convoy moved through streets lined with people on both sides, who stood as though they were waiting for a parade. A few friendly folks from our community waved as we passed by. Some of the white people looked totally horrified, while others raised their fists to us. Others shouted ugly words.

Skill:
Word Patterns and Relationships

I can see that the intensity of the crowd is causing the soldiers to rush. I can infer that the word breakneck means very quickly or rapidly.

14 We pulled up to the front of the school. Groups of soldiers on guard were lined at intervals several feet apart. A group of twenty or more was running at breakneck speed up and down the street in front of Central High School, their rifles with **bayonets** pointed straight ahead. Sarge said they were doing crowd control—keeping the mob away from us.

15 About twenty soldiers moved toward us, forming an olive-drab square with one end open. I glanced at the faces of my friends. Like me, they appeared to be impressed by the **imposing** sight of military power. There was so much to see, and everything was happening so quickly. We walked through the open end of the square. Erect, rifles at their sides, their faces stern, the soldiers did not make eye contact as they surrounded us in a protective cocoon. After a long moment, the leader motioned us to move forward.

16 I felt proud and sad at the same time. Proud that I lived in a country that would go this far to bring justice to a Little Rock girl like me, but sad that they had to go to such great lengths. Yes, this is the United States, I thought to myself. There is a reason that I salute the flag. If these guys just go with us this first time, everything's going to be okay.

17 We began moving forward. The eerie silence of that moment would be forever etched into my memory. All I could hear was my own heartbeat and the sound of boots clicking on the stone.

18 Everyone seemed to be moving in slow motion as I peered past the raised bayonets of the 101st soldiers. I walked on the concrete path toward the front door of the school, the same path the Arkansas National Guard had blocked us from days before. We approached the stairs, our feet moving in unison to the rhythm of the marching click-clack sound of the Screaming Eagles. Step by step we climbed upward—where none of my people had ever before walked as a student. We stepped up the front door of Central High School and crossed the threshold into that place where angry segregationist mobs had forbidden us to go.

Excerpted from *Warriors Don't Cry* by Melba Pattillo Beals, published by Washington Square Press.

First Read

Read "Warriors Don't Cry." After you read, complete the Think Questions below.

 THINK QUESTIONS

1. Refer to one or more details from the text to support your understanding of why soldiers are escorting Beals and other students—both from ideas that are directly stated and ideas that you have inferred from clues in the text.

2. Write two or three sentences exploring how the presence of the students affects different individuals in the crowd in different ways. Cite evidence from the text in your sentences.

3. Cite textual evidence to show how Beals feels about being escorted through the crowds.

4. Use context clues to determine the meaning of the word **distraught** as it is used in *Warriors Don't Cry*. Write your definition of *distraught* here and tell how you found it. Then, use a dictionary to confirm the precise pronunciation of *distraught*.

5. The Latin root *integrat-* most closely means "made whole" or "renewed." Using this information, what do you think the word **integration** means as it is used in paragraph 7? Write your best definition here and explain how you figured it out.

Skill:
Informational Text Structure

Use the Checklist to analyze Informational Text Structure in "Warriors Don't Cry ." Refer to the sample student annotations about Informational Text Structure in the text.

••• CHECKLIST FOR INFORMATIONAL TEXT STRUCTURE

In order to determine the overall structure of a text, note the following:

- ✓ the topic(s) and how the author organizes information about the topic(s)

- ✓ patterns in a paragraph or section of text that reveal the text structure, such as:

  - sequences, including the order of events or steps in a process
  - problems and their solutions
  - cause-and-effect relationships
  - comparisons

- ✓ the overall structure of the text and how each section contributes to the development of ideas

To analyze how a particular sentence, paragraph, chapter, or section fits into the overall structure of a text and contributes to the development of the ideas, use the following questions as a guide:

- ✓ What organizational patterns reveal the text structure the author uses to present information?

- ✓ How does a particular sentence, paragraph, chapter, or section fit into the overall structure of the text? How does it affect the development of the author's ideas?

- ✓ In what ways does the text structure contribute to the development of ideas in the text?

Copyright © BookheadEd Learning, LLC

Please note that excerpts and passages in the StudySync® library and this workbook are intended as touchstones to generate interest in an author's work. The excerpts and passages do not substitute for the reading of entire texts, and StudySync® strongly recommends that students seek out and purchase the whole literary or informational work in order to experience it as the author intended. Links to online resellers are available in our digital library. In addition, complete works may be ordered through an authorized reseller by filling out and returning to StudySync® the order form enclosed in this workbook.

Reading & Writing
Companion

5

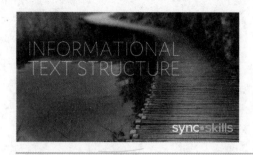

Skill:
Informational Text Structure

Reread paragraphs 17–18 of "Warriors Don't Cry ." Then, using the Checklist on the previous page, answer the multiple-choice questions below.

 YOUR TURN

1. This question has two parts. First, answer Part A. Then, answer Part B.

   Part A: How does the text structure the author uses in the excerpt make one moment particularly effective?

   ○ A. The author uses vivid, sensory details to describe the scene in chronological order.

   ○ B. The author defines the essential qualities of her own heartbeat.

   ○ C. The author discusses the details of moving forward in order of importance.

   ○ D. The author explains how the problem of moving forward was solved.

   Part B: Which of the following details does NOT support your answer to Part A?

   ○ A. "Everyone seemed to be moving in slow motion as I peered past the raised bayonets of the 101st soldiers."

   ○ B. "I walked on the concrete path toward the front door of the school . . ."

   ○ C. ". . . where none of my people had ever before walked as a student."

   ○ D. "We stepped up the front door of Central High School and crossed the threshold . . ."

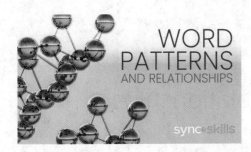

Skill: Word Patterns and Relationships

Use the Checklist to analyze Word Patterns and Relationships in "Warriors Don't Cry." Refer to the sample student annotations about Word Patterns and Relationships in the text.

••• CHECKLIST FOR WORD PATTERNS AND RELATIONSHIPS

In order to determine the relationship between particular words to better understand each of the words, note the following:

- ✓ any unfamiliar words in the text

- ✓ the surrounding words and phrases in order to better understand the meanings or possible relationships between words

- ✓ examples of part/whole, item/category, or other relationships between words, such as cause/effect, where what happens as a result of something

- ✓ the meaning of a word

To use the relationship between particular words to better understand each of the words, consider the following questions:

- ✓ Are these words related to each other in some way? How?

- ✓ What kind of relationship do these words have?

- ✓ Can any of these words be defined by using a part/whole, item/category, or cause/effect relationship?

Please note that excerpts and passages in the StudySync® library and this workbook are intended as touchstones to generate interest in an author's work. The excerpts and passages do not substitute for the reading of entire texts, and StudySync® strongly recommends that students seek out and purchase the whole literary or informational work in order to experience it as the author intended. Links to online resellers are available in our digital library. In addition, complete works may be ordered through an authorized reseller by filling out and returning to StudySync® the order form enclosed in this workbook.

Reading & Writing Companion   7

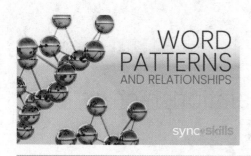

Skill: Word Patterns and Relationships

Reread paragraphs 17–18 from "Warriors Don't Cry." Then, using the Checklist on the previous page, answer the multiple-choice questions below.

↻ YOUR TURN

1. In paragraph 17, the author explains the silence as *eerie*. Then, the author goes on to describe the *eerie* nature of the event in paragraph 18. This is an example of what kind of word relationship?

   ○ A. Cause/effect relationship
   ○ B. Word patterns
   ○ C. Item/category relationship
   ○ D. Part/whole relationship

2. The word *threshold* in paragraph 18 is related to another word or phrase in that sentence through a part/whole relationship. Which word or phrase helps you understand what *threshold* means?

   ○ A. crossed
   ○ B. forbidden
   ○ C. mob
   ○ D. front door

Reading & Writing Companion

Close Read

Reread "Warriors Don't Cry." As you reread, complete the Skills Focus questions below. Then use your answers and annotations from the questions to help you complete the Write activity.

◎ SKILLS FOCUS

1. Identify how Beals uses a chronological text structure to set the scene at the beginning of the excerpt. Explain how details and signal words reveal the text structure.

2. Identify how Beals's description of the order of events on September 25, 1957 contributes to the development of ideas in the text. Explain how details and signal words reveal the text structure.

3. Identify two unknown words in the text and explain how you used word relationships in order to determine their meanings.

4. Highlight evidence in the excerpt that provides details about Beals's personal reaction to events. Explain what Beals wants readers to understand after reading this text.

5. Identify evidence that helps you determine what event Beals is describing in this excerpt from *Warriors Don't Cry* and explain what the event is.

✏ WRITE

INFORMATIONAL: Identify the author's message in the excerpt and describe how the use of a chronological text structure helps her develop that message effectively. Then choose two or three paragraphs from the text and explain the essential **role** that each one plays in the development of ideas in the text. What information does each paragraph contribute to the order of events that Beals describes in her story? Be sure to support your ideas with textual evidence.

Please note that excerpts and passages in the StudySync® library and this workbook are intended as touchstones to generate interest in an author's work. The excerpts and passages do not substitute for the reading of entire texts, and StudySync® strongly recommends that students seek out and purchase the whole literary or informational work in order to experience it as the author intended. Links to online resellers are available in our digital library. In addition, complete works may be ordered through an authorized reseller by filling out and returning to StudySync® the order form enclosed in this workbook.

Reading & Writing Companion   9

Damon and Pythias

DRAMA
Fan Kissen
1964

Introduction

The Greek legend of Damon and Pythias follows the lives of two friends on the island of Sicily. When Pythias is sentenced to death for questioning the cruel laws of their tyrant King, Damon strikes a bargain with the King that puts his life and friendship with Pythias at risk. How much are people really willing to risk for the people they care about? Read the following dramatization of the Greek legend, adapted as a one-act play by author Fan Kissen in 1964.

"There's no telling what a man will do when it's a question of his own life against another's."

CAST OF CHARACTERS

Damon
Pythias
King
Soldier
First Robber
Second Robber
Mother
Narrator
First Voice
Second Voice
Third Voice

1 *(Sound: Iron door opens and shuts. Key in lock.)*

2 *(Music: Up full and out.)*

3 **Narrator.** Long, long ago there lived on the island of Sicily two young men named Damon and Pythias. They were known far and wide for the strong friendship each had for the other. Their names have come down to our own times to mean true friendship. You may hear it said of two persons:

4 **First Voice.** Those two? Why, they're like Damon and Pythias!

5 **Narrator.** The king of that country was a cruel tyrant. He made cruel laws, and he showed no **mercy** toward anyone who broke his laws. Now, you might very well wonder:

6 **Second Voice.** Why didn't the people rebel?

7 **Narrator.** Well, the people didn't dare rebel because they feared the king's great and powerful army. No one dared say a word against the king or his laws—except Damon and Pythias. One day a soldier overheard Pythias speaking against a new law the king had proclaimed.

Skill:
Plot

The play is about two close friends. As I read, I will examine what the characters do and say, and if they change as the plot moves forward.

Skill: Greek and Latin Affixes and Roots

I see a word *unafraid*. I know that the prefix *un-* means "the opposite of." I also know that *afraid* means "scared of." I can infer that *unafraid* means to be brave or not scared.

8 **Soldier.** Ho, there! Who are you that dares to speak so about our king?

9 **Pythias** (*unafraid*) I am called Pythias.

10 **Soldier.** Don't you know it is a crime to speak against the king or his laws? You are under arrest! Come and tell this opinion of yours to the king's face!

11 (*Music: A few short bars in and out.*)

12 **Narrator.** When Pythias was brought before the king, he showed no fear. He stood straight and quiet before the throne.

13 **King.** (*hard, cruel*). So, Pythias! They tell me you do not approve of the laws I make.

14 **Pythias.** I am not alone, Your Majesty, in thinking your laws are cruel. But you rule the people with such an iron hand that they dare not complain.

15 **King** (*angry*). But you have the daring to complain for them! Have they **appointed** you their champion?

16 **Pythias.** No, Your Majesty. I speak for myself alone. I have no wish to make trouble for anyone. But I am not afraid to tell you that the people are suffering under your rule. They want to have a voice in making the laws for themselves. You do not allow them to speak up for themselves.

17 **King.** In other words, you are calling me a tyrant! Well, you shall learn for yourself how a tyrant treats a rebel! Soldier! Throw this man into prison!

18 **Soldier.** At once, Your Majesty! Don't try to resist, Pythias!

19 **Pythias.** I know better than to try to resist a soldier of the king! And for how long am I to remain in prison, Your Majesty, merely for speaking out for the people?

20 **King** (*cruel*). Not for very long, Pythias. Two weeks from today, at noon, you shall be put to death in the public square as an example to anyone else who may dare to question my laws or acts. Off to prison with him, soldier!

21 (*Music: In briefly and out.*)

22 **Narrator.** When Damon heard that his friend Pythias had been thrown into prison and the **severe** punishment that was to follow, he was heartbroken. He rushed to the prison and persuaded the guard to let him speak to his friend.

Skill: Greek and Latin Affixes and Roots

I see the word *persuaded* and I know that it is a verb because Damon is taking action to see his friend Pythian. The root word *suade* means "to urge." I can infer that Damon is trying his hardest to access the jail.

Please note that excerpts and passages in the StudySync® library and this workbook are intended as touchstones to generate interest in an author's work. The excerpts and passages do not substitute for the reading of entire texts, and StudySync® strongly recommends that students seek out and purchase the whole literary or informational work in order to experience it as the author intended. Links to online resellers are available in our digital library. In addition, complete works may be ordered through an authorized reseller by filling out and returning to StudySync® the order form enclosed in this workbook.

23 **Damon.** Oh, Pythias! How terrible to find you here! I wish I could do something to save you!

24 **Pythias.** Nothing can save me, Damon, my dear friend. I am prepared to die. But there is one thought that troubles me greatly.

25 **Damon.** What is it? I will do anything to help you.

26 **Pythias.** I'm worried about what will happen to my mother and my sister when I'm gone.

27 **Damon.** I'll take care of them, Pythias, as if they were my own mother and sister.

28 **Pythias.** Thank you, Damon. I have money to leave them. But there are other things I must arrange. If only I could go to see them before I die! But they live two days' journey from here, you know.

29 **Damon.** I'll go to the king and beg him to give you your freedom for a few days. You'll give your word to return at the end of that time. Everyone in Sicily knows you for a man who has never broken his word.

30 **Pythias.** Do you believe for one moment that the king would let me leave this prison, no matter how good my word may have been all my life?

31 **Damon.** I'll tell him that I shall take your place in this prison cell. I'll tell him that if you do not return by the appointed day, he may kill me in your place!

32 **Pythias.** No, no, Damon! You must not do such a foolish thing! I cannot—I will not—let you do this! Damon! Damon! Don't go! (*to himself*) Damon, my friend! You may find yourself in a cell beside me!

33 (*Music: In briefly and out.*)

34 **Damon** (*begging*). Your Majesty! I beg of you! Let Pythias go home for a few days to bid farewell to his mother and sister. He gives his word that he will return at your appointed time. Everyone knows that his word can be trusted.

35 **King.** In ordinary business affairs—perhaps. But he is now a man under sentence of death. To free him even for a few days would strain his honesty—any man's honesty—too far. Pythias would never return here! I consider him a traitor, but I'm certain he's no fool.

36 **Damon.** Your Majesty! I will take his place in the prison until he comes back. If he does not return, then you may take my life in his place.

Skill:
Plot

Even in conflict, their friendship is strong. Damon will risk his life for Pythias.

37 **King** *(astonished)*. What did you say, Damon?

38 **Damon.** I'm so certain of Pythias that I am offering to die in his place if he fails to return on time.

39 **King.** I can't believe you mean it!

40 **Damon.** I do mean it, Your Majesty.

41 **King.** You make me very curious, Damon, so curious that I'm willing to put you and Pythias to the test. This exchange of prisoners will be made. But Pythias must be back two weeks from today, at noon.

42 **Damon.** Thank you, Your Majesty!

43 **King.** The order with my official seal shall go by your own hand, Damon. But I warn you, if your friend does not return on time, you shall surely die in his place! I shall show no mercy!

44 *(Music: In briefly and out.)*

45 **Narrator.** Pythias did not like the king's bargain with Damon. He did not like to leave his friend in prison with the chance that he might lose his life if something went wrong. But at last Damon persuaded him to leave, and Pythias set out for his home. More than a week went by. The day set for the death sentence drew near. Pythias did not return. Everyone in the city knew of the **condition** on which the king had permitted Pythias to go home. Everywhere people met, the talk was sure to turn to the two friends.

46 **First Voice.** Do you suppose Pythias will come back?

47 **Second Voice.** Why would he stick his head under the king's axe once he's escaped?

48 **Third Voice.** Still, would an honorable man like Pythias let such a good friend die for him?

49 **First Voice.** There's no telling what a man will do when it's a question of his own life against another's.

50 **Second Voice.** But if Pythias doesn't come back before the time is up, he will be killing his friend.

51 **Third Voice.** Well, there's still a few days' time. I, for one, am certain that Pythias will return in time.

52 **Second Voice.** And I am just as certain that he will not. Friendship is friendship, but a man's own life is something stronger, I say!

53 **Narrator.** Two days before the time was up, the king himself visited Damon in his prison cell.

54 *(Sound: Iron door unlocked and opened.)*

55 **King** *(mocking).* You see now, Damon, that you were a fool to make this bargain. Your friend has tricked you! He will not come back here to be killed! He has deserted you!

56 **Damon** *(calm and firm).* I have faith in my friend. I know he will return.

57 **King** *(mocking).* We shall see!

58 *(Sound: Iron door shut and locked.)*

59 **Narrator.** Meanwhile, when Pythias reached the home of his family, he arranged his business affairs so that his mother and sister would be able to live comfortably for the rest of their years. Then he said a last farewell to them before starting back to the city.

60 **Mother** *(in tears).* Pythias, it will take you only two days to get back. Stay another day, I beg you!

61 **Pythias.** I dare not stay longer, Mother. Remember, Damon is locked up in my prison cell while I'm gone. Please don't make it harder for me! Farewell! Don't weep for me. My death may help to bring better days for all our people.

62 **Narrator.** So Pythias began his return journey in plenty of time. But bad luck struck him on the very first day. At twilight, as he walked along a lonely stretch of woodland, a rough voice called:

63 **First Robber.** Not so fast there, young man! Stop!

64 **Pythias** *(startled).* Oh! What is it? What do you want?

65 **Second Robber.** Your money bags.

66 **Pythias.** My money bags? I have only this small bag of coins. I shall need them for some last favors, perhaps, before I die.

67 **First Robber.** What do you mean, before you die? We don't mean to kill you, only to take your money.

Please note that excerpts and passages in the StudySync® library and this workbook are intended as touchstones to generate interest in an author's work. The excerpts and passages do not substitute for the reading of entire texts, and StudySync® strongly recommends that students seek out and purchase the whole literary or informational work in order to experience it as the author intended. Links to online resellers are available in our digital library. In addition, complete works may be ordered through an authorized reseller by filling out and returning to StudySync® the order form enclosed in this workbook.

Reading & Writing Companion   **15**

68 **Pythias.** I'll give you my money, only don't delay me any longer. I am to die by the king's order three days from now. If I don't return to prison on time, my friend must die in my place.

69 **First Robber.** A likely story! What man would be fool enough to go back to prison ready to die?

70 **Second Robber.** And what man would be fool enough to die for you?

71 **First Robber.** We'll take your money, all right. And we'll tie you up while we get away.

72 **Pythias** *(begging)*. No! No! I must get back to free my friend! *(fade)* I must go back!

73 **Narrator.** But the two robbers took Pythias's money, tied him to a tree and went off as fast as they could. Pythias struggled to free himself. He cried out for help as loud as he could for a long time. But no one traveled through that lonesome woodland after dark. The sun had been up for many hours before he finally managed to free himself from the ropes that had tied him to the tree. He lay on the ground, hardly able to breathe.

74 *(Music: In briefly and out.)*

75 **Narrator.** After a while Pythias got to his feet. Weak and dizzy from hunger and thirst and his struggle to free himself, he set off again. Day and night he traveled without stopping, **desperately** trying to reach the city in time to save Damon's life.

76 *(Music: Up and out.)*

77 **Narrator.** On the last day, half an hour before noon, Damon's hands were tied behind his back, and he was taken into the public square. The people muttered angrily as Damon was led in by the jailer. Then the king entered and seated himself on a high platform.

78 *(Sound: Crowd voices in and hold under single voices.)*

79 **Soldier** *(loud)*. Long live the king!

80 **First Voice** *(low)*. The longer he lives, the more miserable our lives will be!

81 **King** *(loud, mocking)*. Well, Damon, your lifetime is nearly up. Where is your good friend Pythias now?

82 **Damon** *(firm)*. I have faith in my friend. If he has not returned, I'm certain it is through no fault of his own.

83 **King** *(mocking)*. The sun is almost overhead. The shadow is almost at the noon mark. And still your friend has not returned to give you back your life!

84 **Damon** *(quiet)*. I am ready, and happy, to die in his place.

85 **King** *(harsh)*. And you shall, Damon! Jailer, lead the prisoner to the—

86 *(Sound: Crowd voices up to a roar, then under.)*

87 **First Voice** *(over noise)*. Look! It's Pythias!

88 **Second Voice** *(over noise)*. Pythias has come back!

89 **Pythias** *(breathless)*. Let me through! Damon!

90 **Damon.** Pythias!

91 **Pythias.** Thank the gods I'm not too late!

92 **Damon** *(quiet, sincere)* I would have died for you gladly, my friend.

93 **Crowd Voices** *(loud, demanding)*. Set them free! Set them both free!

94 **King** (loud). People of the city! *(crowd voices out)* Never in all my life have I seen such faith and friendship, such loyalty between men. There are many among you who call me harsh and cruel. But I cannot kill any man who proves such strong and true friendship for another. Damon and Pythias, I set you both free. *(roar of approval from crowd)* I am king. I command a great army. I have stores of gold and precious jewels. But I would give all my money and my power for one friend like Damon and Pythias!

95 *(Sound: Roar of approval from crowd up briefly and out.)*

96 *(Music: Up and out.)*

ELECTRONIC: © 1964 by Fan Kissen. Reproduced by permission of John Heaslip.

PRINT: "Damon and Pythias" by Fan Kissen, Student Edition. Copyright © 1964, 1949 by Houghton Mifflin Harcourt Publishing Company. All rights reserved. Reproduced by permission of the publisher, Houghton Mifflin Harcourt Publishing Company.

First Read

Read "Damon and Pythias." After you read, complete the Think Questions below.

 THINK QUESTIONS

1. Why does Damon decide to take Pythias's place in jail? Cite specific evidence from the text to support your answer.

2. Why does Pythias not immediately return to Damon? Cite specific evidence from the text to support your answer.

3. What does the king decide to do in the end and why? Cite specific evidence from the text to support your answer.

4. Read the following dictionary entry:

severe
se•vere \sə'vir\

adjective

1. (of something bad) intense
2. (of punishment of a person) strict or harsh

Which definition most closely matches the meaning of **severe** as it is used in the excerpt? Write the correct definition of *severe* here and explain how you figured it out.

5. Use context clues to determine the definition of **desperately** as it used in the text. Then check a print or online dictionary to verify your inferred definition of *desperately*.

PLOT

sync•skills

Skill: Plot

Use the Checklist to analyze Plot in "Damon and Pythias." Refer to the sample student annotations about Plot in the text.

••• CHECKLIST FOR PLOT

In order to determine the plot and how a particular story's or drama's plot unfolds, note the following:

- ✓ specific plot events as they occur in the story

- ✓ series of episodes in the plot

- ✓ ways characters respond or change as the plot moves toward a resolution

- ✓ dialogue between or among characters that reveals their growth or change

To describe how a particular story's or drama's plot unfolds in a series of episodes as well as how the characters respond or change as the plot moves toward a resolution, consider the following questions:

- ✓ What is the plot? What are the key events in the plot?

- ✓ How to the series of episodes in the drama help the plot to unfold ?

- ✓ How do the characters respond or change as the plot moves through the conflict and toward a resolution?

Please note that excerpts and passages in the StudySync® library and this workbook are intended as touchstones to generate interest in an author's work. The excerpts and passages do not substitute for the reading of entire texts, and StudySync® strongly recommends that students seek out and purchase the whole literary or informational work in order to experience it as the author intended. Links to online resellers are available in our digital library. In addition, complete works may be ordered through an authorized reseller by filling out and returning to StudySync® the order form enclosed in this workbook.

Reading & Writing Companion

19

PLOT

Skill:
Plot

Reread paragraphs 79–92 from "Damon and Pythias." Then, using the Checklist on the previous page, answer the multiple-choice questions below.

♺ YOUR TURN

1. In lines 79–83, the king —

   ○ A. prevents Pythias from returning.
   ○ B. frightens Damon by calling the jailer.
   ○ C. is unable to convince Damon that his friend has abandoned him.
   ○ D. convinces Damon his friendship was not as strong as he thought.

2. Which statement best describes the characters Damon and Pythias at the drama's resolution?

   ○ A. They are loyal and have a true friendship.
   ○ B. Their friendship is hard work, but worth it in the end.
   ○ C. Damon and Pythias can't teach the king about friendship.
   ○ D. Damon is affected by wealth and power while Pythias is not.

Reread paragraphs 79–92 of "Damon and Pythias." Then, answer the multiple-choice questions below.

↻ YOUR TURN

1. This question has two parts. First, answer Part A. Then, answer Part B.

   Part A: Based on his last speech, how has the king changed?

   ○ A. He realizes the people think he is harsh and cruel.

   ○ B. The king is ready to give up his wealth to the people.

   ○ C. He has moved from cruelty to understanding.

   ○ D. The king admits he is lonely.

   Part B: Which of the following details BEST supports your answer to Part A?

   ○ A. "There are many among you who call me harsh and cruel."

   ○ B. "Never in all my life have I seen such faith and friendship, such loyalty between men."

   ○ C. "I am king. I command a great army."

   ○ D. "But I cannot kill any man who proves such strong and true friendship for another."

Skill: Greek and Latin Affixes and Roots

Use the Checklist to analyze Greek and Latin Affixes and Roots in "Damon and Pythias." Refer to the sample student annotations about Greek and Latin Affixes and Roots in the text.

••• CHECKLIST FOR GREEK AND LATIN AFFIXES AND ROOTS

In order to identify Greek and Latin affixes and roots, note the following:

- ✓ the root

- ✓ the prefix and/or suffix

To use common, grade-appropriate Greek or Latin affixes and roots as clues to the meaning of a word, use the following questions as a guide:

- ✓ Can I identify the root of this word? Should I look in a dictionary or other resource?

- ✓ What is the meaning of the root?

- ✓ Can I identify the prefix and/or suffix of this word? Should I look in a dictionary or other resource?

- ✓ What is the meaning of the prefix and/or suffix?

- ✓ Does this suffix change the word's part of speech?

- ✓ How do the word parts work together to define the word's meaning and part of speech?

Skill: Greek and Latin Affixes and Roots

Reread lines 75–80 from "Damon and Pythias." Then, using the Checklist on the previous page, answer the multiple-choice questions below.

⟳ YOUR TURN

1. The word *platform* in line 77 is the combination of two words with Greek or Latin roots. *Form* is from the Greek for "shape." Based on context, which of the following do you think is the meaning of *plat*?

   ○ A. small
   ○ B. large
   ○ C. flat
   ○ D. round

2. The Latin word *miserabilis* means "pitiable and wretched." Therefore, the most likely meaning of *miserable* in line 80 is—

   ○ A. unpleasant
   ○ B. majestic
   ○ C. repetitive
   ○ D. uninteresting

Please note that excerpts and passages in the StudySync® library and this workbook are intended as touchstones to generate interest in an author's work. The excerpts and passages do not substitute for the reading of entire texts, and StudySync® strongly recommends that students seek out and purchase the whole literary or informational work in order to experience it as the author intended. Links to online resellers are available in our digital library. In addition, complete works may be ordered through an authorized reseller by filling out and returning to StudySync® the order form enclosed in this workbook.

Reading & Writing Companion   23

Close Read

Reread "Damon and Pythias." As you reread, complete the Skills Focus questions below. Then use your answers and annotations from the questions to help you complete the Write activity.

◎ SKILLS FOCUS

1. Identify a scene that reveals important details about the plot and explain what they are.

2. Highlight evidence in the dialogue that helps you understand who Damon, Pythias, and the king are, and what they want. Explain what you learn about each character.

3. Identify two unknown words in the text that have common Greek or Latin roots or affixes. Explain how you used the roots or affixes to understand the words' meanings.

4. Highlight evidence of how the king changes over the course of the play.

5. Think about the storyline and what it is trying to convey. Then identify evidence in the play that helps you answer the following question: What does the resolution suggest about life in general? Provide an answer based on the evidence.

✏ WRITE

LITERARY ANALYSIS: How do Damon and Pythias respond to conflict as the drama unfolds? Does their friendship ever waver? What do their responses to conflict reveal about their characters? Use evidence and **relevant** examples of dialogue from the text to support your answer.

Amigo Brothers

FICTION

Piri Thomas

1978

Introduction

Piri Thomas (1928–2011) grew up in New York City's rough Spanish Harlem neighborhood and began writing his acclaimed autobiography *Down These Mean Streets* while serving a prison term for attempted robbery. Known for the tough reality portrayed in his works, Thomas's literary output includes memoirs, short stories, essays, and poems. In his story "Amigo Brothers," amateur boxers and best friends Antonio and Felix must fight against each other to determine which one will advance to the Golden Gloves Championship.

"Let's stop a while, bro. I think we both got something to say to each other."

1   Antonio Cruz and Felix Varga were both seventeen years old. They were so together in friendship that they felt themselves to be brothers. They had known each other since childhood, growing up on the lower east side of Manhattan in the same tenement building on Fifth Street between Avenue A and Avenue B.

2   Antonio was fair, lean, and lanky, while Felix was dark, short, and husky. Antonio's hair was always falling over his eyes, while Felix wore his black hair in a natural Afro style.

3   Each youngster had a dream of someday becoming lightweight champion of the world. Every chance they had the boys worked out, sometimes at the Boys Club on 10th Street and Avenue A and sometimes at the pro's gym on 14th Street. Early morning sunrises would find them running along the East River Drive, wrapped in sweat shirts, short towels around their necks, and handkerchiefs Apache style around their foreheads.

4   While some youngsters were into street negatives, Antonio and Felix slept, ate, rapped, and dreamt positive. Between them, they had a collection of *Fight* magazines second to none, plus a scrapbook filled with torn tickets to every boxing match they had ever attended, and some clippings of their own. If asked a question about any given fighter, they would immediately zip out from their memory banks divisions, weights, records of fights, knock-outs, technical knock-outs, and draws or losses.

5   Each had fought many **bouts** representing their community and had won two gold-plated medals plus a silver and bronze medallion. The difference was in their style. Antonio's lean form and long reach made him the better boxer, while Felix's short and muscular frame made him the better slugger. Whenever they had met in the ring for sparring sessions, it had always been hot and heavy.

6   Now, after a series of elimination bouts, they had been informed that they were to meet each other in the division finals that were scheduled for the

Skill:
Character

The friends are different physically and in boxing styles, but both are competitive.

seventh of August, two weeks away—the winner to represent the Boys Club in the Golden Gloves Championship Tournament.

7   The two boys continued to run together along the East River Drive. But even when joking with each other, they both sensed a wall rising between them.

8   One morning less than a week before their bout, they met as usual for their daily work-out. They fooled around with a few jabs at the air, slapped skin, and then took off, running lightly along the dirty East River's edge.

9   Antonio glanced at Felix who kept his eyes purposely straight ahead, pausing from time to time to do some fancy leg work while throwing one-twos followed by upper cuts to an imaginary jaw. Antonio then beat the air with a barrage of body blows and short devastating lefts with an overhand jaw-breaking right.

10   After a mile or so, Felix puffed and said, "Let's stop a while, bro. I think we both got something to say to each other."

11   Antonio nodded. It was not natural to be acting as though nothing unusual was happening when two aceboon buddies were going to be blasting each other within a few short days.

12   They rested their elbows on the railing separating them from the river. Antonio wiped his face with his short towel. The sunrise was now creating day.

13   Felix leaned heavily on the river's railing and stared across to the shores of Brooklyn. Finally, he broke the silence.

14   "Man, I don't know how to come out with it."

15   Antonio helped. "It's about our fight, right?"

16   "Yeah, right." Felix's eyes squinted at the rising orange sun.

17   "I've been thinking about it too, *panin*. In fact, since we found out it was going to be me and you, I've been awake at night, pulling punches on you, trying not to hurt you."

18   "Same here. It ain't natural not to think about the fight. I mean, we both are *cheverote* fighters and we both want to win. But only one of us can win. There ain't no draws in the eliminations."

19   Felix tapped Antonio gently on the shoulder. "I don't mean to sound like I'm bragging, bro. But I wanna win, fair and square."

NOTES

Skill:
Character

These close friends are going to compete against each other. They will both want to win. This will definitely be a conflict.

Please note that excerpts and passages in the StudySync® library and this workbook are intended as touchstones to generate interest in an author's work. The excerpts and passages do not substitute for the reading of entire texts, and StudySync® strongly recommends that students seek out and purchase the whole literary or informational work in order to experience it as the author intended. Links to online resellers are available in our digital library. In addition, complete works may be ordered through an authorized reseller by filling out and returning to StudySync® the order form enclosed in this workbook.

Reading & Writing
Companion   27

20 Antonio nodded quietly. "Yeah. We both know that in the ring the better man wins. Friend or no friend, brother or no . . ."

21 Felix finished it for him. "Brother. Tony, let's promise something right here. Okay?"

22 "If it's fair, *hermano,* I'm for it." Antonio admired the courage of a tug boat pulling a barge five times its welterweight size.

23 "It's fair, Tony. When we get into the ring, it's gotta be like we never met. We gotta be like two heavy strangers that want the same thing and only one can have it. You understand, don'tcha?"

24 "*Si,* I know." Tony smiled. "No pulling punches. We go all the way."

25 "Yeah, that's right. Listen, Tony. Don't you think it's a good idea if we don't see each other until the day of the fight? I'm going to stay with my Aunt Lucy in the Bronx. I can use Gleason's Gym for working out. My manager says he got some sparring partners with more or less your style."

26 Tony scratched his nose **pensively**. "Yeah, it would be better for our heads." He held out his hand, palm upward. "Deal?"

27 "Deal." Felix lightly slapped open skin.

28 "Ready for some more running?" Tony asked lamely.

29 "Naw, bro. Let's cut it here. You go on. I kinda like to get things together in my head."

30 "You ain't worried, are you?" Tony asked.

31 "No way, man." Felix laughed out loud. "I got too much smarts for that. I just think it's cooler if we split right here. After the fight, we can get it together again like nothing ever happened."

32 The amigo brothers were not ashamed to hug each other tightly.

33 "Guess you're right. Watch yourself, Felix. I hear there's some pretty heavy dudes up in the Bronx. *Suavecito,* okay?"

34 "Okay. You watch yourself too, *sabe?*"

35 Tony jogged away. Felix watched his friend disappear from view, throwing rights and lefts. Both fighters had a lot of psyching up to do before the big fight.

36   The days in training passed much too slowly. Although they kept out of each other's way, they were aware of each other's progress via the ghetto grapevine.

37   The evening before the big fight, Tony made his way to the roof of his tenement. In the quiet early dark, he peered over the ledge. Six stories below the lights of the city blinked and the sounds of cars mingled with the curses and the laughter of children in the street. He tried not to think of Felix, feeling he had succeeded in psyching his mind. But only in the ring would he really know. To spare Felix hurt, he would have to knock him out, early and quick.

38   Up in the South Bronx, Felix decided to take in a movie in an effort to keep Antonio's face away from his fists. The flick was *The Champion* with Kirk Douglas, the third time Felix was seeing it.

39   The champion was getting the daylights beat out of him. He was saved only by the sound of the bell.

40   Felix became the champ and Tony the challenger.

41   The movie audience was going out of its head. The champ hunched his shoulders grunting and sniffing red blood back into his broken nose. The challenger, confident that he had the championship in the bag, threw a left. The champ countered with a dynamite right.

42   Felix's right arm felt the shock, Antonio's face, superimposed on the screen, was hit by the awesome force of the blow. Felix saw himself in the ring, blasting Antonio against the ropes. The champ had to be forcibly restrained. The challenger fell slowly to the canvas.

43   When Felix finally left the theatre, he had figured out how to psyche himself for tomorrow's fight. It was Felix the Champion vs. Antonio the Challenger.

44   He walked up some dark streets, deserted except for small pockets of wary-looking kids wearing gang colors.

45   Despite the fact that he was Puerto Rican like them, they eyed him as a stranger to their turf. Felix did a fast shuffle, bobbing and weaving, while letting loose a torrent of blows that would demolish whatever got in its way. It seemed to impress the brothers, who went about their own business.

46   Finding no takers, Felix decided to split to his aunt's. Walking the streets had not relaxed him, neither had the fight flick. All it had done was to stir him up. He let himself quietly into his Aunt Lucy's apartment and went straight to bed, falling into a fitful sleep with sounds of the gong for Round One.

Skill:
Character

Antonio's thoughts show that he has a conflict between wanting to win and valuing his friendship with Felix. Both friends start to change and distance themselves from each other as the story continues.

47 Antonio was passing some heavy time on his rooftop. How would the fight tomorrow **affect** his relationship with Felix? After all, fighting was like any other profession. Friendship had nothing to do with it. A gnawing doubt crept in. He cut negative thinking real quick by doing some speedy fancy dance steps, bobbing and weaving like mercury. The night air was blurred with perpetual motions of left hooks and right crosses. Felix, his *amigo* brother, was not going to be Felix at all in the ring. Just an opponent with another face. Antonio went to sleep, hearing the opening bell for the first round. Like his friend in the South Bronx, he prayed for victory, via a quick clean knock-out in the first round.

48 Large posters plastered all over the walls of local shops announced the fight between Antonio Cruz and Felix Vargas as the main bout.

49 The fight had created great interest in the neighborhood. Antonio and Felix were well liked and respected. Each had his own loyal following.

50 Antonio's fans had unbridled faith in his boxing skills. On the other side, Felix's admirers trusted in his dynamite-packed fists.

51 Felix had returned to his apartment early in the morning of August 7th and stayed there, hoping to avoid seeing Antonio. He turned the radio on to *salsa* music sounds and then tried to read while waiting for word from his manager.

52 The fight was scheduled to take place in Tompkins Square Park. It had been decided that the gymnasium of the Boys Club was not large enough to hold all the people who were sure to attend. In Tompkins Square Park, everyone who wanted could view the fight, whether from ringside or window fire escapes or tenement rooftops.

53 The morning of the fight Tompkins Square was a beehive of activity with numerous workers setting up the ring, the seats, and the guest speakers' stand. The scheduled bouts began shortly after noon and the park had begun filling up even earlier.

Tompkins Square Park in New York City

54 The local junior high school across from Tompkins Square Park served as the dressing room for all the fighters. Each was given a separate classroom with desk tops, covered with mats, serving as resting tables. Antonio thought he caught a glimpse of Felix waving to him from a room at the end of the corridor. He waved back just in case it had been him.

55 The fighters changed from their street clothes into fighting gear. Antonio wore white trunks, black socks, and black shoes. Felix wore sky blue trunks, red socks, and white boxing shoes. Each had dressing gowns to match their fighting trunks with their names neatly stitched on the back.

56 The loudspeakers blared into the open windows of the school. There were speeches by dignitaries, community leaders, and great boxers of yesteryear. Some were well prepared, some **improvised** on the spot. They all carried the same message of great pleasure and honor at being part of such a historic event. This great day was in the tradition of champions **emerging** from the streets of the lower east side.

57 Interwoven with the speeches were the sounds of the other boxing events. After the sixth bout, Felix was much relieved when his trainer Charlie said, "Time change. Quick knock-out. This is it. We're on."

58 Waiting time was over. Felix was escorted from the classroom by a dozen fans in white T-shirts with the word FELIX across their fronts.

59 Antonio was escorted down a different stairwell and guided through a roped-off path.

60 As the two climbed into the ring, the crowd exploded with a roar. Antonio and Felix both bowed gracefully and then raised their arms in acknowledgment.

61 Antonio tried to be cool, but even as the roar was in its first birth, he turned slowly to meet Felix's eyes looking directly into his. Felix nodded his head and Antonio responded. And both as one, just as quickly, turned away to face his own corner.

62 Bong—bong—bong. The roar turned to stillness.

63 "Ladies and Gentlemen, *Señores y Señoras*."

64 The announcer spoke slowly, pleased at his bilingual efforts.

65 "Now the moment we have all been waiting for—the main event between two fine young Puerto Rican fighters, products of our lower east side.

66 "In this corner, weighing 134 pounds, Felix Vargas. And in this corner, weighing 133 pounds, Antonio Cruz. The winner will represent the Boys Club in the tournament of champions, the Golden Gloves. There will be no draw. May the best man win."

NOTES

67   The cheering of the crowd shook the window panes of the old buildings surrounding Tompkins Square Park. At the center of the ring, the referee was giving instructions to the youngsters.

68   "Keep your punches up. No low blows. No punching on the back of the head. Keep your heads up. Understand. Let's have a clean fight. Now shake hands and come out fighting."

69   Both youngsters touched gloves and nodded. They turned and danced quickly to their corners. Their head towels and dressing gowns were lifted neatly from their shoulders by their trainers' nimble fingers. Antonio crossed himself. Felix did the same.

70   BONG! BONG! ROUND ONE. Felix and Antonio turned and faced each other squarely in a fighting pose. Felix wasted no time. He came in fast, head low, half hunched toward his right shoulder, and lashed out with a straight left. He missed a right cross as Antonio slipped the punch and countered with one-two-three lefts that snapped Felix's head back, sending a mild shock coursing through him. If Felix had any small doubt about their friendship affecting their fight, it was being neatly dispelled.

71   Antonio danced, a joy to behold. His left hand was like a piston pumping jabs one right after another with seeming ease. Felix bobbed and weaved and never stopped boring in. He knew that at long range he was at a disadvantage. Antonio had too much reach on him. Only by coming in close could Felix hope to achieve the dreamed-of knockout.

72   Antonio knew the dynamite that was stored in his *amigo* brother's fist. He ducked a short right and missed a left hook. Felix trapped him against the ropes just long enough to pour some punishing rights and lefts to Antonio's hard midsection. Antonio slipped away from Felix, crashing two lefts to his head, which set Felix's right ear to ringing.

73   Bong! Both *amigos* froze a punch well on its way, sending up a roar of approval for good sportsmanship.

74   Felix walked briskly back to his corner. His right ear had not stopped ringing. Antonio gracefully danced his way toward his stool none the worse, except for glowing glove burns, showing angry red against the whiteness of his midribs.

75   "Watch that right, Tony." His trainer talked into his ear. "Remember Felix always goes to the body. He'll want you to drop your hands for his overhand left or right. Got it?"

Copyright © BookheadEd Learning, LLC

76   Antonio nodded, spraying water out between his teeth. He felt better as his sore midsection was being firmly rubbed.

77   Felix's corner was also busy.

78   "You gotta get in there, fella." Felix's trainer poured water over his curly Afro locks. "Get in there or he's gonna chop you up from way back."

79   *Bong! Bong!* Round two. Felix was off his stool and rushed Antonio like a bull, sending a hard right to his head. Beads of water exploded from Antonio's long hair.

80   Antonio, hurt, sent back a blurring barrage of lefts and rights that only meant pain to Felix, who returned with a short left to the head followed by a looping right to the body. Antonio countered with his own flurry, forcing Felix to give ground. But not for long.

81   Felix bobbed and weaved, bobbed and weaved, occasionally punching his two gloves together.

82   Antonio waited for the rush that was sure to come. Felix closed in and feinted with his left shoulder and threw his right instead. Lights suddenly exploded inside Felix's head as Antonio slipped the blow and hit him with a pistonlike left, catching him flush on the point of his chin.

83   Badlam broke loose as Felix's legs momentarily buckled. He fought off a series of rights and lefts and came back with a strong right that taught Antonio respect.

84   Antonio danced in carefully. He knew Felix had the habit of playing possum when hurt, to sucker an opponent within reach of the powerful bombs he carried in each fist.

85   A right to the head slowed Antonio's pretty dancing. He answered with his own left at Felix's right eye that began puffing up within three seconds.

86   Antonio, a bit too eager, moved in too close and Felix had him entangled into a rip-roaring, punching toe-to-toe slugfest that brought the whole Tompkins Square Park screaming to its feet.

87   Rights to the body. Lefts to the head. Neither fighter was giving an inch. Suddenly a short right caught Antonio squarely on the chin. His long legs turned to jelly and his arms flailed out desperately. Felix, grunting like a bull, threw wild punches from every direction. Antonio, groggy, bobbed and

weaved, evading most of the blows. Suddenly his head cleared. His left flashed out hard and straight catching Felix on the bridge of his nose.

88 Felix lashed back with a haymaker, right off the ghetto streets. At the same instant, his eye caught another left hook from Antonio. Felix swung out trying to clear the pain. Only the frenzied screaming of those along the ringside let him know that he had dropped Antonio. Fighting off the growing haze, Antonio struggled to his feet, got up, ducked, and threw a smashing right that dropped Felix flat on his back.

89 Felix got up as fast as he could in his own corner, groggy but still game. He didn't even hear the count. In a fog, he heard the roaring of the crowd, who seemed to have gone insane. His head cleared to hear the bell sound at the end of the round. He was very glad. His trainer sat him down on the stool.

90 In his corner, Antonio was doing what all fighters do when they are hurt. They sit and smile at everyone.

91 The referee signaled the ring doctor to check the fighters outs. He did so and then gave his okay. The cold water sponges brought **clarity** to both *amigo* brothers. They were rubbed until their circulation ran free.

92 *Bong!* Round three—the final round. Up to now it had been tic-tac-toe, pretty much even. But everyone knew there could be no draw and that this round would decide the winner.

93 This time, to Felix's surprise, it was Antonio who came out fast, charging across the ring. Felix braced himself but couldn't ward off the barrage of punches. Antonio drove Felix hard against the ropes.

94 The crowd ate it up. Thus far the two had fought with *mucho corazón*. Felix tapped his gloves and commenced his attack anew. Antonio, throwing boxer's caution to the winds, jumped in to meet him.

95 Both pounded away. Neither gave an inch and neither fell to the canvas. Felix's left eye was tightly closed. Claret red blood poured from Antonio's nose. They fought toe-to-toe.

96 The sounds of their blows were loud in contrast to the silence of a crowd gone completely mute.

97 *Bong! Bong! Bong!* The bell sounded over and over again. Felix and Antonio were past hearing. Their blows continued to pound on each other like hailstones.

98   Finally the referee and the two trainers pried Felix and Antonio apart. Cold water was poured over them to bring them back to their senses.

99   They looked around and then rushed toward each other. A cry of alarm surged through Tompkins Square Park. Was this a fight to the death instead of a boxing match?

100   The fear soon gave way to wave upon wave of cheering as the two *amigos* embraced.

101   No matter what the decision, they knew they would always be champions to each other.

102   *BONG! BONG! BONG!* "Ladies and Gentlemen. *Señores* and *Señoras*. The winner and representative to the Golden Gloves Tournament of Champions is . . ."

103   The announcer turned to point to the winner and found himself alone. Arm in arm the champions had already left the ring.

© 1978 by Piri Thomas, STORIES FROM EL BARRIO. Reproduced by permission of the Trust of Piri J. Thomas and Suzanne Dod Thomas

Please note that excerpts and passages in the StudySync® library and this workbook are intended as touchstones to generate interest in an author's work. The excerpts and passages do not substitute for the reading of entire texts, and StudySync® strongly recommends that students seek out and purchase the whole literary or informational work in order to experience it as the author intended. Links to online resellers are available in our digital library. In addition, complete works may be ordered through an authorized reseller by filling out and returning to StudySync® the order form enclosed in this workbook.

Reading & Writing Companion   **35**

First Read

Read "Amigo Brothers." After you read, complete the Think Questions below.

☁ THINK QUESTIONS

1. Why does the narrator refer to Antonio Cruz and Felix Varga as the "amigo brothers"? How are the boys alike? How are they different? Cite specific evidence from paragraphs 1–3 to support your answer.

2. How does the reader know that boxing is important to Antonio and Felix? Cite specific evidence from paragraphs 3 and 4 to support your response.

3. Why is the upcoming division match a challenge for Antonio and Felix's friendship? Explain how the boys share a similar point of view about the match. Cite specific evidence from paragraphs 11–25 to support your response.

4. Use context clues to determine the meaning of the word **pensively** as it is used in paragraph 26.

5. The Latin word *imprōvīsus* means "unforeseen" or "unexpected." Use this information to infer the meaning of the word **improvised** as it appears in paragraph 56 of the text. Write your best definition here and explain how you figured it out.

Skill:
Character

Use the Checklist to analyze Character in "Amigo Brothers." Refer to the sample student annotations about Character in the text.

••• CHECKLIST FOR CHARACTER

In order to determine how the characters respond or change as the plot moves toward a resolution, note the following:

✓ the characters in the story, including the protagonist and antagonist

✓ key events among the series of episodes in the plot, especially events that cause characters to react, respond, or change in some way

✓ characters' responses as the plot reaches a climax, and moves toward a resolution of the problem facing the protagonist

✓ the resolution of the conflict in the plot and the ways it affects each character

To describe how the plot of a particular story or drama unfolds in a series of episodes as well as how the characters respond or change as the plot moves toward a resolution, consider the following questions:

✓ How do the characters' responses change or develop from the beginning to the end of the story?

✓ Do the characters in the story change? Which event or events in the story causes a character to change?

✓ Is there an event in the story that provokes, or causes, a character to make a decision?

✓ Do the characters' problems reach a resolution? How?

✓ How does the resolution affect the characters?

Skill:
Character

Reread paragraphs 97–103 from "Amigo Brothers." Then, using the Checklist on the previous page, answer the multiple-choice questions below.

↻ YOUR TURN

1. Based on how Felix and Antonio act in paragraphs 97 through 99 after the bell sounds, the reader can conclude that —

   ○ A. the audience wants them to keep fighting.
   ○ B. each boy is overtaken by the desire to win.
   ○ C. the boys hate each other.
   ○ D. they are both sweaty.

2. The author's description of the event and what it means in paragraphs 99 and 100 reveals that the boys —

   ○ A. choose their friendship over winning.
   ○ B. are ready to hear the announcer name the winner.
   ○ C. realize they are endangering each other.
   ○ D. are badly injured and about to collapse.

3. The boys' final act in the last paragraph show that they —

   ○ A. need medical help.
   ○ B. have given up boxing.
   ○ C. think they are both winners.
   ○ D. do not want to be champions.

Close Read

Reread "Amigo Brothers." As you reread, complete the Skills Focus questions below. Then use your answers and annotations from the questions to help you complete the Write activity.

◎ SKILLS FOCUS

1. Think about the responses that Antonio and Felix have to events in the story. How do these responses both slowly reveal their individual characters and also help to develop the plot? Write a response to this question, citing evidence from the text to support your claim.

2. Highlight evidence that reveals how Antonio and Felix are similar and different. Explain how these similarities and differences affect the story's plot.

3. Identify details in the text that show how Antonio and Felix's relationship changes over the course of the story. Explain how these details help you infer a theme.

4. Identify and summarize the events of the story in a way that maintains meaning and logical order.

5. Identify evidence in "Amigo Brothers" that reveals the central conflict the two characters face. Explain what the conflict is.

✏ WRITE

LITERARY ANALYSIS: What efforts do Antonio and Felix make to achieve their dreams? What do their efforts reveal about them? In what ways are Antonio and Felix **similar** to and different from each other? How do they change as the plot moves toward a resolution? Write a response to these questions, citing evidence from the text to support your answers.

Please note that excerpts and passages in the StudySync® library and this workbook are intended as touchstones to generate interest in an author's work. The excerpts and passages do not substitute for the reading of entire texts, and StudySync® strongly recommends that students seek out and purchase the whole literary or informational work in order to experience it as the author intended. Links to online resellers are available in our digital library. In addition, complete works may be ordered through an authorized reseller by filling out and returning to StudySync® the order form enclosed in this workbook,

Reading & Writing Companion   **39**

Listen, Slowly

FICTION
Thanhhà Lai
2015

Introduction

The second novel by author Thanhhà Lai (b. 1965) introduces readers to an American-born Vietnamese family. Twelve-year-old Mai—who wants nothing more than to vacation with friends in Laguna Beach over the summer—is asked to accompany her grandmother, Bà, to Vietnam to figure out if her grandfather is still alive. In this excerpt, Mai is still adjusting to life in the Vietnamese village when Bà begins to open up about her past.

"Bà understands; she always has."

1   We're under the mosquito net again, getting ready for a nap. After being force-fed at breakfast and lunch today, we're tired. I was made to eat so much sticky rice and mung beans, my belly feels like it's packed with bricks. I'm still burping, trying to digest it all.

2   The net is supposed to be used only at night but I wouldn't let Bà roll ours up. Mosquitoes hunt from dusk to dawn, but I bet there are some who stretch the hours. I feel safer inside the net, lying here and scratching like I have fleas. Bà has already told me scratching only makes it worse. If I ignore the itches, according to her, soon my blood will no longer **react** to the poison. This mind-over-matter thing has never worked for me.

3   I've thought about playing up the mosquito angle, maybe scratch myself bloody, moan a lot, shake like I have malaria. That might get me airlifted to Laguna. But doctors back home would run tests and figure out I faked the whole thing and Mom would ship me right back, probably for the entire summer. So I've got to suck it up and wait for the detective to bring the guard. Then Bà can ask all her questions. Tears. Acceptance. Incense. Home. Not much else can happen.

4   Bà pulls out her Tiger Balm. Bad, bad sign. How could I have forgotten about her cure-all weapon? I stop scratching and forbid myself to touch even one pink bump, but it's too late. Bà is twisting open the shiny metal lid and reaching out for me. Why did I have to call attention to myself? She holds up my right arm and **meticulously** rubs the ointment on each pink dot. You know what a minty, burning, menthol-y goo does to mosquito bites? It makes them itch even more! But I can't reason with Bà about Tiger Balm, which she has **anointed** with the power to blast away headaches, backaches, joint aches, stomachaches, nausea, seasickness, carsickness, burns, bites, gas, congestions . . . just to name a few.

5   Now Bà wants my other arm. Noooo. I quickly stick my finger into the jar, scoop out a **pungent** gob and pretend to rub it on my bites. I'm actually massaging it on the flat skin surrounding the bumps. Even so, it burns. Bà waits for me to assault my calves and ankles and feet and neck and face. My

Skill:
Language, Style
and Audience

I can tell that the narrator is not happy to be with her grandmother. She would rather scratch herself, bleed and pretend to have a disease! Her tone sounds sarcastic and she seems selfish.

eyes have turned into waterfalls. Tiger Balm is no joke. Finally, Bà closes the lid.

6   *"Guess what once floated on that wall?"* Bà asks. I always understand whatever Bà says because she uses only the words she has taught me.

7   Through stinging eyes, I kinda see that on the wall used to be a mural, made of blue tiles. Most have fallen off, leaving pockmarks on the dingy wall. Everything in the house is cracked and gray. Outside, the year *1929* is carved into the wood above the doorway. Bà said Ông was born that year and, to celebrate, his father designed a house inspired by his travels: one story, tile roof, brick walls, windows facing every direction, rooms that extend out instead of up, and a garden that claimed much more land than the house itself.

8   I suddenly remember the word for blue, *"Xanh."*

9   *"Yes. Remember our stories about the goddess in a blue robe that drifts like tea vapors? Remnants of her gown still remain."*

10 I do remember, smiling big to show Bà. Twice a day I used to hear long stories, one at nap time and one before bed. Then I went to kindergarten and stopped listening.

11 *"I have known Ông since the beginning of memories, matched as one from his seventh year, my fifth. Marriage to be delayed until he had studied in France, I in Japan. Yet war reached us. We were joined at eighteen, sixteen. Too soon. The day of our wedding people arrived at our door. They bore drums and flags and silver gift trays covered in red velvet. The first two days proved simple to hide from him, so many relatives, so many ceremonies. But the third day, four men with muscles like twisted laundry carried me in a palanquin to his parents' door. As taught, I took steps light as a crane's into the house, bowed before the ancestral altar. While everyone prayed, I retreated inside the first room with a door.*

12 *"This one. The bridal chamber. In pink silk a bed floated, from above a blue goddess gazed. I pushed an armoire against the door and sat on the floor counting the thumps from my heart. Out there they pleaded, then threatened, then my father thundered. Yet, I sat. The season was spring. Peach petals drifted outside the open window. I jumped up. Too late. Ông was perched on the windowsill, having climbed the peach tree. I pushed him back and slammed the bamboo shutters. His shape showed through, even the hint of curls by his ears. His voice seeped through too. Ah, that voice. In such a voice, sharp tones shattered and landed in drops of bells. He talked until the*

sun shriveled to an orange-yellow seed. He talked until I released the shutters.

13   *"For years now, I've counted the hours I had lost, that day and days after, when I was reading or visiting relatives or daydreaming, hours I could have been beside him. For years, I've counted the hours ever after as I wait for some part of him to return to me. I'm no dreamer. Raising seven children during war has a way of slapping reality into one's fate. And yet, against reason, I continue to wait."*

14   *"Ông sống?"* Ông alive? I suck in a huge breath, willing this to be the right moment to ask. I softly squeeze Bà's hand to mean I've been thinking about this for some time.

15   Bà understands; she always has. I don't know how, but Bà has always known how I feel at any given moment, especially when I'm sad, especially when I'm in need of a quartered lemon drop.

16   *"I do not live on butterfly wings, my child. His chances of remaining among us rank as likely as finding an ebony orchid. Yet I hold on to hope because I have been unable to imagine his ending. If intact, he would have returned to this room. We promised should life separate us, we would rejoin under the blue goddess. He never returned to us, but he never truly departed. I came here knowing I will unlikely be granted him in person, but perhaps I will be allowed to reclaim something of his, anything at all. The guard knows how Ông spent his days, what he ate, what he wore, what he said, the weight in his eyes, the shade of his skin, the whistle of his breaths. I need to absorb every morsel deemed knowable, then I have* **vowed** *to release the heaviness of longing."*

17   Bà lets go of my hand and turns from me. Time to let her rest.

18   My body loosens and expands, remembering how it used to make room for her words to wiggle deep into the tiny crevices along my bones, muscles, and joints. Becoming a part of me. I've always been able to imagine her as a rich girl who grew up in wartime and ended up raising seven children alone. She always says, *"Cờ đến tay, phải phất."* Flag in hand, you must wave it. It wasn't about being brave or extraordinary so much as inhaling all the way to her core and accepting her responsibilities.

19   But I have never understood how she got through her loss. How do you know someone almost since birth, then one day you know absolutely nothing more about him at all? Ông made plans, she told me, plans of how to educate their children, how to care for their parents, how to wait for peace, how to behave in old age. They did not plan on being apart after he was thirty-seven and she

Skill: Language, Style and Audience

Ba's tone seems melancholy; she misses her husband. She regrets the time they had apart and wishes she could be with him now. I feel badly for her when I read this, but also hopeful that she's still waiting for him.

thirty-five. I used to think that was old, but that was much younger than Mom and Dad now.

20   Bà has fallen asleep. Her snores will deepen. I roll toward her and inhale Tiger Balm mixed with BenGay, all the way down to my toes. The most tingly, comforting scent there is.

Excerpted from Listen, Slowly by Thanhha Lai, published by HarperCollins.

First Read

Read "Listen, Slowly." After you read, complete the Think Questions below.

 THINK QUESTIONS

1. What inferences can you make about Mai's character from the first four paragraphs? Cite evidence from the text to support your response.

2. What is the significance of the blue tiles on the wall to Bà? Use evidence from the text to support your response.

3. How has Mai's perspective changed by the end of the excerpt? Cite evidence from the text to support your response.

4. The Latin word *pungens* means "to sting." Use this information to help infer the meaning of the word **pungent** as it appears in paragraph 5. Write your best definition of *pungent* here and explain how you figured it out.

5. Use context clues to determine the meaning of the word **vowed** as it is used in paragraph 16. Write your best definition of *vowed* here and explain how you figured out its meaning.

Please note that excerpts and passages in the StudySync® library and this workbook are intended as touchstones to generate interest in an author's work. The excerpts and passages do not substitute for the reading of entire texts, and StudySync® strongly recommends that students seek out and purchase the whole literary or informational work in order to experience it as the author intended. Links to online resellers are available in our digital library. In addition, complete works may be ordered through an authorized reseller by filling out and returning to StudySync® the order form enclosed in this workbook.

Reading & Writing Companion   45

Skill:
Language, Style, and Audience

Use the Checklist to analyze Language, Style, and Audience in "Listen, Slowly." Refer to the sample student annotations about Language, Style, and Audience in the text.

••• CHECKLIST FOR LANGUAGE, STYLE, AND AUDIENCE

In order to determine an author's style, do the following:

✓ identify and define any unfamiliar words or phrases

✓ use context, including the meaning of surrounding words and phrases

✓ note possible reactions to the author's word choice

✓ examine your reaction to the author's word choice, and how the author's choice affected your reaction

To analyze the impact of specific word choice on meaning and tone, ask the following questions:

✓ How did your understanding of the language change during your analysis?

✓ What stylistic choices can you identify in the text? How does the style influence your understanding of the language?

✓ How could various audiences interpret this language? What possible different emotional responses can you list?

✓ How does the writer's choice of words impact or create a specific tone in the text?

Skill:
Language, Style, and Audience

Reread paragraphs 19–20 from "Listen, Slowly." Then, using the Checklist on the previous page, answer the multiple-choice questions below.

⟳ YOUR TURN

1. What does the author's tone and word choice in paragraph 19 reveal about how Mai feels about her grandmother?

    ○ A. she is angry with her grandmother

    ○ B. she has empathy for her and admires her strength

    ○ C. she misses her grandfather as well

    ○ D. she is upset her grandmother made her come to Vietnam

2. Which of the following words best describes Mai's attitude toward her grandmother's lotions (paragraph 20)?

    ○ A. dislike

    ○ B. afraid

    ○ C. calming

    ○ D. excited

LISTEN, SLOWLY

Close Read

Reread "Listen, Slowly." As you reread, complete the Skills Focus questions below. Then use your answers and annotations from the questions to help you complete the Write activity.

◎ SKILLS FOCUS

1. Figurative language is language used for descriptive effect. Identify evidence of how the author uses figurative language to develop the personalities of the characters. Explain what the figurative language tells you about the characters.

2. Identify places where the author uses specific word choice or tone to create Mai's voice. Explain how this language helps you understand Mai's feelings.

3. Identify places in the text where the author uses words or phrases to express Bà's personality. Explain what these words or phrases tell you about Bà as a character.

4. Highlight evidence that suggests that Mai is interested in Bà's story and is brought closer to her by their conversation. Explain your reasoning.

✏ WRITE

LITERARY ANALYSIS: How does the author use language to develop the audience's understanding of Mai and Bà? What does their conversation in the excerpt say about them as **individuals** and as family members? Cite evidence from the text to support your response.

Charles

FICTION
Shirley Jackson
1948

Introduction

Shirley Jackson (1916–1965) was a popular and prolific writer in her short life. Before her death at age 48, she published six novels, two memoirs, four children's books, and a collection of short stories. Her two best known works are "The Lottery" and *The Haunting of Hill House*, which was nominated for the National Book Award and has been described by bestselling horror writer Stephen King as one of the "two great novels of the supernatural in the last hundred years." "Charles" follows in the suspense-and-twist tradition of the controversial and often-anthologized short story, "The Lottery," whose haunting incident takes place on June 27th—a day forever named Shirley Jackson Day in the author's

"Well, Charles was bad again today."

Skill:
Point of View

The phrase "my son"
says that the narrator
is Laurie's mother. She
uses the pronouns my,
I, and me, so the story
is told in the first
person. The reader
knows and sees only
what the narrator
describes.

1   The day my son Laurie started kindergarten he **renounced** corduroy overalls with bibs and began wearing blue jeans with a belt; I watched him go off the first morning with the older girl next door, seeing clearly that an era of my life was ended, my sweet-voiced nursery-school tot replaced by a long-trousered, swaggering character who forgot to stop at the corner and wave good-bye to me.

2   He came running home the same way, the front door slamming open, his cap on the floor, and the voice suddenly become raucous shouting, "Isn't anybody *here*?"

3   At lunch he spoke insolently to his father, spilled his baby sister's milk, and remarked that his teacher said we were not to take the name of the Lord in vain.

4   "How *was* school today?" I asked, **elaborately** casual.

5   "All right," he said.

6   "Did you learn anything?" his father asked.

7   Laurie regarded his father coldly. "I didn't learn nothing," he said.

8   "Anything," I said. "Didn't learn anything."

9   "The teacher spanked a boy, though," Laurie said, **addressing** his bread and butter.

10   "For being fresh," he added, with his mouth full.

11   "What did he do?" I asked. "Who was it?"

12   Laurie thought. "It was Charles," he said. "He was fresh. The teacher spanked him and made him stand in the corner. He was awfully fresh."

NOTES

13   "What did he do?" I asked again, but Laurie slid off his chair, took a cookie, and left, while his father was still saying, "See here, young man."

14   The next day Laurie remarked at lunch, as soon as he sat down, "Well, Charles was bad again today." He grinned enormously and said, "Today Charles hit the teacher."

15   "Good heavens," I said, mindful of the Lord's name, "I suppose he got spanked again?"

16   "He sure did," Laurie said. "Look up," he said to his father.

17   "What?" his father said, looking up.

18   "Look down," Laurie said. "Look at my thumb. Gee, you're dumb." He began to laugh insanely.

19   "Why did Charles hit the teacher?" I asked quickly.

20   "Because she tried to make him color with red crayons," Laurie said. "Charles wanted to color with green crayons so he hit the teacher and she spanked him and said nobody play with Charles but everybody did."

21   The third day—it was a Wednesday of the first week—Charles bounced a see-saw on to the head of a little girl and made her bleed, and the teacher made him stay inside all during recess. Thursday Charles had to stand in a corner during story-time because he kept pounding his feet on the floor. Friday Charles was **deprived** of black-board privileges because he threw chalk.

22   On Saturday I remarked to my husband, "Do you think kindergarten is too unsettling for Laurie? All this toughness and bad grammar, and this Charles boy sounds like such a bad influence."

23   "It'll be alright," my husband said reassuringly. "Bound to be people like Charles in the world. Might as well meet them now as later."

24   On Monday Laurie came home late, full of news. "Charles," he shouted as he came up the hill; I was waiting **anxiously** on the front steps. "Charles," Laurie yelled all the way up the hill, "Charles was bad again."

25   "Come right in," I said, as soon as he came close enough. "Lunch is waiting."

26   "You know what Charles did?" he demanded, following me through the door. "Charles yelled so in school they sent a boy in from first grade to tell the

Skill:
Point of View

The narrator reveals that she feels anxious, or nervous, waiting for Laurie. She only knows what has happened from what Laurie says. This limits the point of view.

Please note that excerpts and passages in the StudySync® library and this workbook are intended as touchstones to generate interest in an author's work. The excerpts and passages do not substitute for the reading of entire texts, and StudySync® strongly recommends that students seek out and purchase the whole literary or informational work in order to experience it as the author intended. Links to online resellers are available in our digital library. In addition, complete works may be ordered through an authorized reseller by filling out and returning to StudySync® the order form enclosed in this workbook.

Reading & Writing Companion   51

teacher she had to make Charles keep quiet, and so Charles had to stay after school. And so all the children stayed to watch him."

27 "What did he do?" I asked.

28 "He just sat there," Laurie said, climbing into his chair at the table. "Hi, Pop, y'old dust mop."

29 "Charles had to stay after school today," I told my husband. "Everyone stayed with him."

30 "What does this Charles look like?" my husband asked Laurie. "What's his other name?"

31 "He's bigger than me," Laurie said. "And he doesn't have any rubbers and he doesn't wear a jacket."

32 Monday night was the first Parent-Teachers meeting, and only the fact that the baby had a cold kept me from going; I wanted passionately to meet Charles's mother. On Tuesday Laurie remarked suddenly, "Our teacher had a friend come to see her in school today."

33 "Charles's mother?" my husband and I asked simultaneously.

34 "Naaah," Laurie said scornfully. "It was a man who came and made us do exercises, we had to touch our toes. Look." He climbed down from his chair and squatted down and touched his toes. "Like this," he said. He got solemnly back into his chair and said, picking up his fork, "Charles didn't even *do* exercises."

35 "That's fine," I said heartily. "Didn't Charles want to do exercises?"

36 "Naaah," Laurie said. "Charles was so fresh to the teacher's friend he wasn't *let* do exercises."

37 "Fresh again?" I said.

38 "He kicked the teacher's friend," Laurie said. "The teacher's friend just told Charles to touch his toes like I just did and Charles kicked him."

39 "What are they going to do about Charles, do you suppose?" Laurie's father asked him.

40 Laurie shrugged elaborately. "Throw him out of school, I guess," he said.

41 Wednesday and Thursday were routine; Charles yelled during story hour and hit a boy in the stomach and made him cry. On Friday Charles stayed after school again and so did all the other children.

42 With the third week of kindergarten Charles was an institution in our family; the baby was being a Charles when she cried all afternoon; Laurie did a Charles when he filled his wagon full of mud and pulled it through the kitchen; even my husband, when he caught his elbow in the telephone cord and pulled the telephone and a bowl of flowers off the table, said, after the first minute, "Looks like Charles."

43 During the third and fourth weeks it looked like a reformation in Charles; Laurie reported grimly at lunch on Thursday of the third week, "Charles was so good today the teacher gave him an apple."

44 "What?" I said, and my husband added warily, "You mean Charles?"

45 "Charles," Laurie said. "He gave the crayons around and he picked up the books afterward and the teacher said he was her helper."

46 "What happened?" I asked incredulously.

47 "He was her helper, that's all," Laurie said, and shrugged.

48 "Can this be true about Charles?" I asked my husband that night. "Can something like this happen?"

49 "Wait and see," my husband said cynically. "When you've got a Charles to deal with, this may mean he's only plotting." He seemed to be wrong. For over a week Charles was the teacher's helper; each day he handed things out and he picked things up; no one had to stay after school.

50 "The PTA meeting's next week again," I told my husband one evening. "I'm going to find Charles's mother there."

51 "Ask her what happened to Charles," my husband said. "I'd like to know."

52 "I'd like to know myself," I said.

53 On Friday of that week things were back to normal. "You know what Charles did today?" Laurie demanded at the lunch table, in a voice slightly awed. "He told a little girl to say a word and she said it and the teacher washed her mouth out with soap and Charles laughed."

54 "What word?" his father asked unwisely, and Laurie said, "I'll have to whisper it to you, it's so bad." He got down off his chair and went around to his father.

NOTES

His father bent his head down and Laurie whispered joyfully. His father's eyes widened.

55 "Did Charles tell the little girl to say *that*?" he asked respectfully.

56 "She said it *twice*," Laurie said. "Charles told her to say it *twice*."

57 "What happened to Charles?" my husband asked.

58 "Nothing," Laurie said. "He was passing out the crayons."

59 Monday morning Charles abandoned the little girl and said the evil word himself three or four times, getting his mouth washed out with soap each time. He also threw chalk.

60 My husband came to the door with me that evening as I set out for the PTA meeting. "Invite her over for a cup of tea after the meeting," he said. "I want to get a look at her."

61 "If only she's there." I said prayerfully.

62 "She'll be there," my husband said. "I don't see how they could hold a PTA meeting without Charles's mother."

63 At the meeting I sat restlessly, scanning each comfortable matronly face, trying to determine which one hid the secret of Charles. None of them looked to me haggard enough. No one stood up in the meeting and apologized for the way her son had been acting. No one mentioned Charles.

64 After the meeting I identified and sought out Laurie's kindergarten teacher. She had a plate with a cup of tea and a piece of chocolate cake; I had a plate with a cup of tea and a piece of marshmallow cake. We maneuvered up to one another cautiously, and smiled.

65 "I've been so anxious to meet you," I said. "I'm Laurie's mother."

66 "We're all so interested in Laurie," she said.

67 "Well, he certainly likes kindergarten," I said. "He talks about it all the time."

68 "We had a little trouble **adjusting**, the first week or so," she said primly, "but now he's a fine helper. With occasional lapses, of course."

69 "Laurie usually adjusts very quickly," I said. "I suppose this time it's Charles's influence."

70 "Charles?"

71 "Yes," I said, laughing, "you must have your hands full in that kindergarten, with Charles."

72 "Charles?" she said. "We don't have any Charles in the kindergarten."

Please note that excerpts and passages in the StudySync® library and this workbook are intended as touchstones to generate interest in an author's work. The excerpts and passages do not substitute for the reading of entire texts, and StudySync® strongly recommends that students seek out and purchase the whole literary or informational work in order to experience it as the author intended. Links to online resellers are available in our digital library. In addition, complete works may be ordered through an authorized reseller by filling out and returning to StudySync® the order form enclosed in this workbook.

Reading & Writing Companion 55

CHARLES

First Read

Read "Charles." After you read, complete the Think Questions below.

☁ THINK QUESTIONS

1. How does Laurie's behavior suddenly change when he leaves for his first day of kindergarten? Cite textual evidence from the selection to support your answer.

2. Write two or three sentences describing how Charles, as Laurie tells it, disrupts the kindergarten classroom during the first week of school.

3. Why is the narrator scanning each "comfortable matronly face" at the PTA meeting? Be sure to use textual evidence in your response.

4. Read the following dictionary entry:

   address ad•dress \ə'dres\
   noun

   1. the number and street of a residence or business
   2. a speech delivered before an audience or crowd

   verb

   1. to deal with or direct efforts toward
   2. to speak to an audience

   Addressing is the present participle form of the verb *address*. Which definition of *address* most closely matches the meaning of *addressing* as it is used in paragraph 9? Write the correct definition of *addressing* here and explain how you figured out the correct meaning.

5. Which context clues help you determine the meaning of **deprived** as it is used in paragraph 21 of "Charles"? Write your own definition of *deprived* and explain which words or phrases helped you understand its meaning.

Skill:
Point of View

Use the Checklist to analyze Point of View in "Charles." Refer to the sample student annotations about Point of View in the text.

••• CHECKLIST FOR POINT OF VIEW

In order to identify the point of view of the narrator or speaker in a text, note the following:

✓ the speaker(s) or narrator(s)

✓ how much the narrator(s) or speaker(s) knows and reveals

✓ what the narrator(s) or speaker(s) says or does that reveals how he or she feels about other characters and events in the poem or story

To explain how an author develops the point of view of the narrator or speaker in a text, consider the following questions:

✓ Is the narrator or speaker objective or does he or she mislead the reader? How?

✓ What is the narrator's or the speaker's point of view?

- Is the narrator or speaker "all-knowing," or omniscient?

- Is the narrator or speaker limited to revealing the thoughts and feelings of one character?

- Are there multiple narrators or speakers telling the story?

✓ How does the narrator or speaker reveal his or her thoughts about the events or the other characters in the story or poem? How does the narrator's or speaker's experiences and cultural background affect his or her thoughts?

Please note that excerpts and passages in the StudySync® library and this workbook are intended as touchstones to generate interest in an author's work. The excerpts and passages do not substitute for the reading of entire texts, and StudySync® strongly recommends that students seek out and purchase the whole literary or informational work in order to experience it as the author intended. Links to online resellers are available in our digital library. In addition, complete works may be ordered through an authorized reseller by filling out and returning to StudySync® the order form enclosed in this workbook.

Reading & Writing Companion   57

Skill:
Point of View

Reread paragraphs 63–72 of "Charles." Then, using the Checklist on the previous page, answer the multiple-choice questions below.

⟳ YOUR TURN

1. This question has two parts. First, answer Part A. Then, answer Part B.

   Part A What does the story's ending reveal about the first-person point of view of the narrator?

   ○ A. The narrator is confused by the teacher's final statement.

   ○ B. The narrator knew that Laurie was misbehaving.

   ○ C. The narrator didn't know that Charles wasn't real or that it was her child who was misbehaving.

   ○ D. The narrator knew that Charles wasn't real the whole time.

   Part B How would the story be different if told from a third-person omniscient point of view?

   ○ A. Readers would have known all along that Charles was Laurie since they would know all the characters' thoughts and feelings.

   ○ B. Readers would be observers who experience the story through one character, so they would find out that Charles was Laurie at the same time as the narrator.

   ○ C. The author would address readers directly to explain that Charles wasn't real.

   ○ D. Readers would be able to identify closely with the teacher's viewpoint.

Close Read

Reread "Charles." As you reread, complete the Skills Focus questions below. Then use your answers and annotations from the questions to help you complete the Write activity.

◎ SKILLS FOCUS

1. Highlight evidence that indicates from which point of view "Charles" is told. Explain what the point of view is and why you think the author selected it.

2. Identify **specific** evidence in the story that shows how the narrator's limited point of view affects her description of characters or events.

3. A character's personality consists of the traits that make the character different from others, such as whether the character is honest or devious. Highlight examples of Laurie's words and actions that reveal his personality. Explain how these words or actions help develop the plot.

4. When you summarize a text, you state the main ideas or events and the most important details in your own words. Highlight events in the story that are central to the plot. Then summarize the most important events in your own words.

5. Laurie's tales about Charles are central to the story. Highlight evidence that shows how Laurie's feelings about Charles change over the course of the story. Explain what this tells you about Laurie.

✏ WRITE

ARGUMENTATIVE: At the end of "Charles," the reader and the narrator both learn that the title character is a person who is unknown to the teacher. This suggests that Laurie's mother, the narrator, has a limited point of view. Therefore, what exactly has been going on throughout Laurie's first weeks of kindergarten? What clues, if any, are presented that the narrator overlooks? Develop an argument in which you state what you think has actually happened in the story and whether you think that the narrator should have known all along that Laurie was lying to her.

Please note that excerpts and passages in the StudySync® library and this workbook are intended as touchstones to generate interest in an author's work. The excerpts and passages do not substitute for the reading of entire texts, and StudySync® strongly recommends that students seek out and purchase the whole literary or informational work in order to experience it as the author intended. Links to online resellers are available in our digital library. In addition, complete works may be ordered through an authorized reseller by filling out and returning to StudySync® the order form enclosed in this workbook.

Reading & Writing Companion   **59**

Saying
Yes

POETRY
Diana Chang
1974

Introduction

Author of nine books, 20th-century author and professor Diana Chang (b. 1934) is considered to be the first Chinese American to publish a novel in the United States. As a trailblazing writer and a New Yorker who also lived in Nanjing, Shanghai, and Beijing, Chang's poem "Saying Yes" most likely emerged from autobiographical roots.

"Are you Chinese?"
"Yes."
"American?"
"Yes."

NOTES

1 "Are you Chinese?"
2 "Yes."

3 "American?"
4 "Yes."

5 "Really Chinese?"
6 "No . . . not **quite**."

7 "Really American?"
8 "Well, actually, you see . . ."

9 But I would **rather** say
10 yes
11 Not neither-nor,
12 not maybe,
13 but both, and not only

14 The homes I've had,
15 the ways I am

16 I'd rather say it twice,
17 yes

© 1974 by Diana Chang. Reproduced by permission of Kacie Chang.

WRITE

PERSONAL RESPONSE: Have you ever been asked a question about yourself that was impossible to give a yes or no answer to? Use Chang's poem as a model for inspiration and write a lyrical conversation in Chang's style. It can be autobiographical or entirely imagined. As in Chang's poem, be sure to include lines of dialogue at the beginning and a concluding stance at the end that makes it clear what your poem's speaker really wants to say. Title your poem either "Saying Yes" or "Saying No."

The All-American Slurp

FICTION
Lensey Namioka
1987

Introduction

Prolific young adult author Lensey Namioka (b. 1929) emigrated from China to the United States when she was nine years old. She often writes with levity about Chinese and Japanese families and themes of Americanization. Her short story, "The All-American Slurp," follows a family that finds the true proving

"The Gleasons' dinner party wasn't so different from a Chinese meal after all."

Skill:
Setting

From the details in this paragraph, I can tell that the story takes place in America and that the characters are new to the country. Being new to a place might create a conflict in the story.

1 The first time our family was invited out to dinner in America, we disgraced ourselves while eating celery. We had emigrated to this country from China, and during our early days here we had a hard time with American table manners.

2 In China we never ate celery raw, or any other kind of vegetable raw. We always had to disinfect the vegetables in boiling water first. When we were presented with our first relish tray, the raw celery caught us unprepared.

3 We had been invited to dinner by our neighbors, the Gleasons. After arriving at the house, we shook hands with our hosts and packed ourselves into a sofa. As our family of four sat stiffly in a row, my younger brother and I stole glances at our parents for a clue as to what to do next.

4 Mrs. Gleason offered the relish tray to Mother. The tray looked pretty, with its tiny red radishes, curly sticks of carrots, and long, slender stalks of pale green celery. "Do try some of the celery, Mrs. Lin," she said. "It's from a local farmer, and it's sweet."

5 Mother picked up one of the green stalks, and Father followed suit. Then I picked up a stalk, and my brother did too. So there we sat, each with a stalk of celery in our right hand.

6 Mrs. Gleason kept smiling. "Would you like to try some of the dip, Mrs. Lin? It's my own recipe: sour cream and onion flakes, with a dash of Tabasco sauce."

7 Most Chinese don't care for dairy products, and in those days I wasn't even ready to drink fresh milk. Sour cream sounded perfectly revolting. Our family shook our heads in unison.

8 Mrs. Gleason went off with the relish tray to the other guests, and we carefully watched to see what they did. Everyone seemed to eat the raw vegetables quite happily.

9 Mother took a bite of her celery. *Crunch.* "It's not bad!" she whispered.

10 Father took a bite of his celery. *Crunch.* "Yes, it *is* good," he said, looking surprised.

11 I took a bite, and then my brother. *Crunch, crunch.* It was more than good; it was delicious. Raw celery has a slight sparkle, a zingy taste that you don't get in cooked celery. When Mrs. Gleason came around with the relish tray, we each took another stalk of celery, except my brother. He took two.

12 There was only one problem: long strings ran through the length of the stalk, and they got caught in my teeth. When I help my mother in the kitchen, I always pull the strings out before slicing celery.

13 I pulled the strings out of my stalk. *Z-z-zip, z-z-zip.* My brother followed suit. *Z-z-zip, z-z-zip.* To my left, my parents were taking care of their own stalks. *Z-z-zip, z-z-zip, z-z-zip.*

14 Suddenly I realized that there was dead silence except for our zipping. Looking up, I saw that the eyes of everyone in the room were on our family. Mr. and Mrs. Gleason, their daughter Meg, who was my friend, and their neighbors the Badels—they were all staring at us as we busily pulled the strings off our celery.

15 That wasn't the end of it. Mrs. Gleason announced that dinner was served and invited us to the dining table. It was **lavishly** covered with platters of food, but we couldn't see any chairs around the table. So we helpfully carried over some dining chairs and sat down. All the other guests just stood there. Mrs. Gleason bent down and whispered to us, "This is a buffet dinner. You help yourselves to some food and eat it in the living room."

16 Our family beat a retreat back to the sofa as if chased by enemy soldiers. For the rest of the evening, too **mortified** to go back to the dining table, I nursed a bit of potato salad on my plate.

17 Next day Meg and I got on the school bus together. I wasn't sure how she would feel about me after the spectacle our family made at the party. But she was just the same as usual, and the only reference she made to the party was, "Hope you and your folks got enough to eat last night. You certainly didn't take very much. Mom never tries to figure out how much food to prepare. She just puts everything on the table and hopes for the best."

18 I began to relax. The Gleasons' dinner party wasn't so different from a Chinese meal after all. My mother also puts everything on the table and hopes for the best.

• • •

19 Meg was the first friend I had made after we came to America. I eventually got acquainted with a few other kids in school, but Meg was still the only real friend I had.

20 My brother didn't have any problems making friends. He spent all his time with some boys who were teaching him baseball, and in no time he could speak English much faster than I could—not better, but faster.

21 I worried more about making mistakes, and I spoke carefully, making sure I could say everything right before opening my mouth. At least I had a better accent than my parents, who never really got rid of their Chinese accent, even years later. My parents had both studied English in school before coming to America, but what they had studied was mostly written English, not spoken.

22 Father's approach to English was a scientific one. Since Chinese verbs have no tense, he was fascinated by the way English verbs changed form according to whether they were in the present, past imperfect, perfect, pluperfect, future, or future perfect tense. He was always making diagrams of verbs and their inflections, and he looked for opportunities to show off his mastery of the pluperfect and future perfect tenses, his two favorites. "I shall have finished my project by Monday," he would say smugly.

23 Mother's approach was to memorize lists of polite phrases that would cover all possible social situations. She was constantly muttering things like "I'm fine, thank you. And you?" Once she accidentally stepped on someone's foot and hurriedly blurted, "Oh that's quite all right!" Embarrassed by her slip, she **resolved** to do better next time. So when someone stepped on *her* foot, she cried, "You're welcome!"

24 In our own different ways, we made progress in learning English. But I had another worry, and that was my appearance. My brother didn't have to worry, since Mother bought him blue jeans for school, and he dressed like all the other boys. But she insisted that girls had to wear skirts. By the time she saw that Meg and the other girls were wearing jeans, it was too late. My school clothes were bought already, and we didn't have money left to buy new outfits for me. We had too many other things to buy first, like furniture, pots, and pans.

25 The first time I visited Meg's house, she took me upstairs to her room, and I wound up trying on her clothes. We were pretty much the same size, since Meg was shorter and thinner than average. Maybe that's how we became friends in the first place. Wearing Meg's jeans and T-shirt, I looked at myself in the mirror. I could almost pass for an American—from the back, anyway. At

least the kids in school wouldn't stop and stare at me in the hallways, which was what they did when they saw me in my white blouse and navy blue skirt that went a couple of inches below the knees.

26 When Meg came to my house, I invited her to try on my Chinese dresses, the ones with a high collar and slits up the sides. Meg's eyes were bright as she looked at herself in the mirror. She struck several sultry poses, and we nearly fell over laughing.

• • •

27 The dinner party at the Gleasons' didn't stop my growing friendship with Meg. Things were getting better for me in other ways too. Mother finally bought me some jeans at the end of the month, when father got his paycheck. She wasn't in any hurry about buying them at first, until I worked on her. This is what I did. Since we didn't have a car in those days, I often ran down to the neighborhood store to pick up things for her. The groceries cost less at a big supermarket, but the closest one was many blocks away. One day, when she ran out of flour, I offered to borrow a bike from our neighbor's son and buy a ten-pound bag of flour at the big supermarket. I mounted the boy's bike and waved to my Mother. "I'll be back in five minutes!"

28 Before I started pedaling, I heard her voice behind me. "You can't go out in public like that! People can see all the way up your thighs!"

29 "I'm sorry," I said innocently. "I thought you were in a hurry to get the flour." For dinner we were going to have pot-stickers (fried Chinese dumplings), and we needed a lot of flour.

pot-stickers (fried Chinese dumplings)

30 "Couldn't you borrow a girl's bicycle?" complained Mother. "That way your skirt won't be pushed up."

31 "There aren't too many of those around," I said. "Almost all the girls wear jeans while riding a bike, so they don't see any point in buying a girl's bike."

32 We didn't eat pot-stickers that evening, and Mother was thoughtful. Next day we took the bus downtown and she bought me a pair of jeans. In the same week, my brother made the baseball team of his junior high school, Father started taking driving lessons, and Mother discovered rummage sales. We soon got all the furniture we needed, plus a dartboard and a 1,000-piece jigsaw puzzle (fourteen hours later, we discovered that it was a 999-piece

Please note that excerpts and passages in the StudySync® library and this workbook are intended as touchstones to generate interest in an author's work. The excerpts and passages do not substitute for the reading of entire texts, and StudySync® strongly recommends that students seek out and purchase the whole literary or informational work in order to experience it as the author intended. Links to online resellers are available in our digital library. In addition, complete works may be ordered through an authorized reseller by filling out and returning to StudySync® the order form enclosed in this workbook.

Reading & Writing Companion   67

jigsaw puzzle). There was hope that the Lins might become a normal American family after all.

. . .

Skill:
Setting

These details tell me that the Lakeview restaurant is a very formal place. I think the Lin family might feel nervous or unsure about what to do in this setting.

33 Then came our dinner at the Lakeview restaurant.

34 The Lakeview was an expensive restaurant, one of those places where a head waiter dressed in tails **conducted** you to your seat, and the only light came from candles and flaming desserts. In one corner of the room a lady harpist played tinkling melodies.

35 Father wanted to celebrate, because he had just been promoted. He worked for an electronics company, and after his English started improving, his superiors decided to appoint him to a position more suited to his training. The promotion not only brought a higher salary but was also a tremendous boost to his pride.

36 Up to then we had eaten only in Chinese restaurants. Although my brother and I were becoming fond of hamburgers, my parents didn't care much for western food, other than chow mein.

37 But this was a special occasion, and father asked his coworkers to recommend a really elegant restaurant. So there we were at the Lakeview, stumbling after the headwaiter in the murky dining room.

38 At our table we were handed our menus, and they were so big that to read mine I almost had to stand up again. But why bother? It was mostly in French, anyway.

39 Father, being an engineer, was always systematic. He took out a pocket French dictionary. "They told me that most of the items would be in French, so I came prepared." He even had a pocket flashlight, the size of a marking pen. While mother held the flashlight over the menu, he looked up the items that were in French.

40 "*Paté en croute*," he muttered. "Let's see . . . *paté* is paste . . . *croute* is crust . . . hmm . . . a paste in crust."

41 The waiter stood looking patient. I squirmed and died at least fifty times.

42 At long last Father gave up. "Why don't we just order four complete dinners at random?" he suggested.

43 "Isn't that risky?" asked Mother. "The French eat some rather peculiar things, I've heard."

44   "A Chinese can eat anything a Frenchman can eat," Father declared.

45   The soup arrived in a plate. How do you get soup up from a plate? I glanced at the other diners, but the ones at the nearby tables were not on their soup course, while the more distant ones were invisible in the darkness.

46   Fortunately my parents had studied books on western etiquette before they came to America. "Tilt your plate," whispered my mother. "It's easier to spoon the soup up that way."

47   She was right. Tilting the plate did the trick. But the etiquette book didn't say anything about what you did after the soup reached your lips. As any respectable Chinese knows, the correct way to eat your soup is to slurp. This helps to cool the liquid and prevent you from burning your lips. It also shows your appreciation.

48   We showed our appreciation. *Shloop*, went my father. *Shloop*, went my mother. *Shloop, shloop*, went my brother, who was the hungriest.

49   The lady harpist stopped playing to take a rest. And in the silence, our family's consumption of soup suddenly seemed unnaturally loud. You know how it sounds on a rocky beach when the tide goes out and the water drains from all those little pools? They go *shloop, shloop, shloop*. That was the Lin family, eating soup.

50   At the next table a waiter was pouring wine. When a large *shloop* reached him, he froze. The bottle continued to pour, and red wine flooded the tabletop and into the lap of a customer. Even the customer didn't notice anything at first, being also hypnotized by the *shloop, shloop, shloop*.

51   It was too much. "I need to go to the toilet," I mumbled, jumping to my feet. A waiter, sensing my urgency, quickly directed me to the ladies' room.

52   I splashed cold water on my burning face, and as I dried myself with a paper towel, I stared into the mirror. In this perfumed ladies' room, with its pink and silver wallpaper and marbled sinks, I looked completely out of place. What was I doing here? What was our family doing in the Lakeview restaurant? In America?

53   The door to the ladies' room opened. A woman came in and glanced **curiously** at me. I retreated into one of the toilet cubicles and latched the door.

54   Time passed—maybe half an hour, maybe an hour. Then I heard the door open again, and my mother's voice. "Are you in there? You're not sick, are you?"

55 There was real concern in her voice. A girl can't leave her family just because they slurp their soup. Besides, the toilet cubicle had a few drawbacks as a permanent residence. "I'm all right," I said, undoing the latch.

56 Mother didn't tell me how the rest of the dinner went, and I didn't want to know. In the weeks following, I managed to push the whole thing into the back of my mind, where it jumped out at me only a few times a day. Even now, I turn hot all over when I think of the Lakeview restaurant.

. . .

57 But by the time we had been in this country for three months, our family was definitely making progress toward becoming Americanized. I remember my parents' first PTA meeting. Father wore a neat suit and tie, and Mother put on her first pair of high heels. She stumbled only once. They met my homeroom teacher and beamed as she told them that I would make honor roll soon at the rate I was going. Of course Chinese etiquette forced Father to say that I was a very stupid girl and Mother to protest that the teacher was showing favoritism toward me. But I could tell they were both very proud.

. . .

58 The day came when my parents announced that they wanted to give a dinner party. We had invited Chinese friends to eat with us before, but this dinner was going to be different. In addition to a Chinese-American family, we were going to invite the Gleasons.

59 "Gee, I can hardly wait to have dinner at your house," Meg said to me. "I just *love* Chinese food."

60 That was a relief. Mother was a good cook, but I wasn't sure if people who ate sour cream would also eat chicken gizzards stewed in soy sauce.

61 Mother decided not to take a chance with the chicken gizzards. Since we had western guests, she set the table with large dinner plates, which we never used in Chinese meals. In fact we didn't use individual plates at all, but picked up food from the platters in the middle of the table and brought it directly to our rice bowls. Following the practice of Chinese-American restaurants, Mother also placed large serving spoons on the platters.

62 The dinner started well. Mrs. Gleason exclaimed at the beautifully arranged dishes of food: the colorful candied fruit in the sweet-and-sour pork dish, the noodle-thin shreds of chicken meat stir-fried with tiny peas, and the glistening pink prawns in a ginger sauce.

NOTES

63   At first I was too busy enjoying my food to notice how the guests were doing. But soon I remembered my duties. Sometimes guests were too polite to help themselves and you had to serve them with more food.

64   I glanced at Meg, to see if she needed more food, and my eyes nearly popped out at the sight of her plate. It was piled with food: the sweet-and-sour meat pushed right against the chicken shreds, and the chicken sauce ran into the prawns. She had been taking food from a second dish before she finished eating her helping from the first!

65   Horrified, I turned to look at Mrs. Gleason. She was dumping rice out of her bowl and putting it on her dinner plate. Then she ladled prawns and gravy on top of the rice and mixed everything together, the way you mix sand, gravel, and cement to make concrete.

66   I couldn't bear to look any longer, and I turned to Mr. Gleason. He was chasing a pea around his plate. Several times he got it to the edge, but when he tried to pick it up with his chopsticks, it rolled back to the center of the plate again. Finally, he put down his chopsticks and picked up the pea with his fingers. He really did! A grown man!

67   All of us, our family and the Chinese guests, stopped eating to watch the activities of the Gleasons. I wanted to giggle. Then I caught my mother's eyes on me. She frowned and shook her head slightly, and I understood the message: the Gleasons were not used to Chinese ways, and they were just coping the best they could. For some reason I thought of celery strings.

68   When the main courses were finished, mother brought out a platter of fruit. " I hope you weren't expecting a sweet dessert," she said. " Since the Chinese don't eat dessert, I didn't think to prepare any."

69   "Oh, I couldn't possibly eat dessert!" cried Mrs. Gleason. "I'm simply stuffed!"

70   Meg had different ideas. When the table was cleared, she announced that she and I were going for a walk. "I don't know about you, but I feel like dessert," she told me, when we were outside. "Come on, there's a Dairy Queen down the street. I could use a big chocolate milkshake!"

71   Although I didn't really want anything more to eat, I insisted on paying for the milkshakes. After all, I was still hostess.

72   Meg got her large chocolate milkshake and I had a small one. Even so, she was finishing hers while I was only half done. Toward the end she pulled hard on her straw and went *shloop, shloop*.

73 "Do you always slurp when you eat a milkshake?" I asked before I could stop myself.

74 Meg grinned. "Sure. All Americans slurp."

THE ALL-AMERICAN SLURP

First Read

Read "The All-American Slurp." After you read, complete the Think Questions below.

☁ THINK QUESTIONS

1. What problems does the narrator's family have when they go to dinner at their neighbors, the Gleasons? Cite textual evidence to support your answer.

2. How do the members of the narrator's family each tackle the problems that come from trying to learn English in their own way? Cite specific evidence from the text to support your answer.

3. At the Chinese dinner the narrator's family prepares for their neighbors, what happens that surprises the narrator? Cite specific evidence from the text to support your answer.

4. Read the following dictionary entry:

mortify

mor•ti•fy \môrdəˌfī\

verb

1. to make someone feel shame or embarrassment
2. to control or suppress by will

Which definition most closely matches the meaning of **mortified** in paragraph 16? Write the correct definition of *mortified* here and explain how you figured it out.

5. Use context clues to determine the meaning of the word **conducted** as it is used in paragraph 34. Write your best definition of *conducted* here and explain how you inferred its meaning.

Please note that excerpts and passages in the StudySync® library and this workbook are intended as touchstones to generate interest in an author's work. The excerpts and passages do not substitute for the reading of entire texts, and StudySync® strongly recommends that students seek out and purchase the whole literary or informational work in order to experience it as the author intended. Links to online resellers are available in our digital library. In addition, complete works may be ordered through an authorized reseller by filling out and returning to StudySync® the order form enclosed in this workbook.

Reading & Writing Companion 73

Skill:
Setting

Use the Checklist to analyze Setting in "The All-American Slurp." Refer to the sample student annotations about Setting in the text.

In order to identify how the plot of a particular story or drama unfolds in a series of episodes, note the following:

✓ key elements in the plot

✓ the setting(s) in the story

✓ how the plot unfolds in a series of episodes

✓ how the setting shapes the plot

To describe how the plot of a particular story or drama unfolds in a series of episodes, consider the following questions:

✓ When and where does this story take place?

✓ How does the plot unfold in a series of episodes?

✓ How does the setting affect the plot? How does it affect the characters and their responses to events? How does the setting help move the plot to a resolution?

Skill: Setting

Reread paragraphs 14–18 from "The All-American Slurp." Then, using the Checklist on the previous page, answer the multiple-choice questions below.

⟳ YOUR TURN

1. Based on paragraph 16, the reader can conclude that —

   ○ A. the Lin family feels out of place in the Gleasons' house.

   ○ B. the Lin family feels comfortable in the Gleasons' house.

   ○ C. the Lin family enjoys buffet-style dining.

   ○ D. the Lin family hates dinner parties.

2. How does the setting influence the Lin family's behavior in the excerpt?

   ○ A. The Lins are overly excited to eat dinner at the Gleasons' house, which is why they behave strangely.

   ○ B. The Lins are glad to finally become friends with an American family.

   ○ C. The Lins are unsure how to behave at the Gleasons' dinner party, which is why they make a few embarrassing mistakes.

   ○ D. The Lins are disgusted by American food.

3. Which paragraph shows the similarities between the narrator's family and Meg's family?

   ○ A. 14

   ○ B. 15

   ○ C. 16

   ○ D. 18

Please note that excerpts and passages in the StudySync® library and this workbook are intended as touchstones to generate interest in an author's work. The excerpts and passages do not substitute for the reading of entire texts, and StudySync® strongly recommends that students seek out and purchase the whole literary or informational work in order to experience it as the author intended. Links to online resellers are available in our digital library. In addition, complete works may be ordered through an authorized reseller by filling out and returning to StudySync® the order form enclosed in this workbook.

Reading & Writing Companion   75

THE ALL-AMERICAN SLURP

Close Read

Reread "The All-American Slurp." As you reread, complete the Skills Focus questions below. Then use your answers and annotations from the questions to help you complete the Write activity.

◎ SKILLS FOCUS

1. Identify how the immigrant experience of learning English affects each character as the story's plot unfolds.

2. Identify how the two dinner parties in the story shape the plot, using **specific** examples from these events in your response.

3. The theme of Lensey Namioka's story is the blending of cultures. Identify evidence that suggests what the narrator learns about culture when she catches Meg slurping her milkshake.

4. In "Saying Yes," the speaker claims to be a part of two cultures. Identify ways in which the narrator in "The All-American Slurp" is also part of two cultures.

5. In "Saying Yes," the speaker tells the story of her identity. She describes how others often ask her to define herself. In "The All-American Slurp," identify evidence that suggests how the narrator would answer the same questions about Chinese and American identity.

✏ WRITE

DISCUSSION: "Saying Yes" and "The All-American Slurp" both feature **distinct** cultural settings. How does each text make use of Chinese and American cultures to influence the development of plot and character? Compare and contrast the relationships between setting, plot, and character in the two texts. Remember to support your ideas with evidence from the texts. In a discussion with your peers, use evidence from both texts as well as personal experience to respond to these questions.

Helen Keller

POETRY
Langston Hughes
1931

Introduction

The fiction and poetry of Missouri-born Langston Hughes (1902–1967) has resonated with readers for generations. As one of the leading figures of a literary movement known as the Harlem Renaissance, Hughes typically wrote about African-American experiences and struggles. In this poem, however, he turns his attention to a Southern white woman who also faced a great struggle: Helen Keller. Deaf and blind from a young age, Keller overcame her physical limitations to become a beloved author and activist.

"She,
Within herself,
Found loveliness . . ."

1 She,
2 In the dark,
3 Found light
4 Brighter than many ever see.
5 She,
6 Within herself,
7 Found loveliness,
8 Through the soul's own **mastery.**
9 And now the world receives
10 From her **dower:**
11 The message of the strength
12 Of inner power.

ELECTRONIC:

PRINT:

WRITE

PERSONAL RESPONSE: The speaker of the poem says of Helen Keller that "She,/ Within herself,/ Found loveliness,/ Through the soul's own mastery." What does it mean to find something "within" yourself? When a person faces a challenge, why might it be necessary to turn inward rather than look for answers from other people or the outside world? In a personal response, record your conclusions. Include examples from the poem and your own prior experience to support your conclusions.

Please note that excerpts and passages in the StudySync® library and this workbook are intended as touchstones to generate interest in an author's work. The excerpts and passages do not substitute for the reading of entire texts, and StudySync® strongly recommends that students seek out and purchase the whole literary or informational work in order to experience it as the author intended. Links to online resellers are available in our digital library. In addition, complete works may be ordered through an authorized reseller by filling out and returning to StudySync® the order form enclosed in this workbook.

Reading & Writing Companion   **79**

The Story of My Life
(Chapter IV)

INFORMATIONAL TEXT
Helen Keller
1903

Introduction

Serious illness at the age of nineteen months left Helen Keller both blind and deaf. Serving as an inspiration to millions, Keller overcame those handicaps and went on to become a renowned author and social activist. In this passage from her autobiography, six-year-old Helen meets the person who will change her life forever, her private teacher Anne Sullivan.

"I did not know what the future held of marvel or surprise for me."

NOTES

Excerpt from Chapter IV

1   The most important day I remember in all my life is the one on which my teacher, Anne Mansfield Sullivan, came to me. I am filled with wonder when I consider the immeasurable contrasts between the two lives which it connects. It was the third of March, 1887, three months before I was seven years old.

Helen Keller with her teacher, Anne Mansfield Sullivan

2   On the afternoon of that eventful day, I stood on the porch, dumb, expectant. I guessed vaguely from my mother's signs and from the hurrying to and fro in the house that something unusual was about to happen, so I went to the door and waited on the steps. The afternoon sun penetrated the mass of honeysuckle that covered the porch, and fell on my upturned face. My fingers lingered almost unconsciously on the familiar leaves and blossoms which had just come forth to greet the sweet southern spring. I did not know what the future held of marvel or surprise for me. Anger and bitterness had preyed upon me continually for weeks and a deep languor had succeeded this passionate struggle.

3   Have you ever been at sea in a dense fog, when it seemed as if a tangible white darkness shut you in, and the great ship, tense and anxious, **groped** her way toward the shore with plummet and sounding-line, and you waited with beating heart for something to happen? I was like that ship before my education began, only I was without compass or sounding-line, and had no way of knowing how near the harbour was. "Light! give me light!" was the wordless cry of my soul, and the light of love shone on me in that very hour.

4   I felt approaching footsteps. I stretched out my hand as I supposed to my mother. Some one took it, and I was caught up and held close in the arms of

her who had come to **reveal** all things to me, and, more than all things else, to love me.

5　The morning after my teacher came she led me into her room and gave me a doll. The little blind children at the Perkins **Institution** had sent it and Laura Bridgman had dressed it; but I did not know this until afterward. When I had played with it a little while, Miss Sullivan slowly spelled into my hand the word "d-o-l-l." I was at once interested in this finger play and tried to imitate it. When I finally succeeded in making the letters correctly I was flushed with childish pleasure and pride. Running downstairs to my mother I held up my hand and made the letters for doll. I did not know that I was spelling a word or even that words existed; I was simply making my fingers go in monkey-like imitation. In the days that followed I learned to spell in this uncomprehending way a great many words, among them pin, hat, cup and a few verbs like sit, stand and walk. But my teacher had been with me several weeks before I understood that everything has a name.

6　One day, while I was playing with my new doll, Miss Sullivan put my big rag doll into my lap also, spelled "d-o-l-l" and tried to make me understand that "d-o-l-l" applied to both. Earlier in the day we had had a tussle over the words "m-u-g" and "w-a-t-e-r." Miss Sullivan had tried to impress it upon me that "m-u-g" is mug and that "w-a-t-e-r" is water, but I persisted in **confounding** the two. In despair she had dropped the subject for the time, only to renew it at the first opportunity. I became impatient at her repeated attempts and, seizing the new doll, I dashed it upon the floor. I was keenly delighted when I felt the fragments of the broken doll at my feet. Neither sorrow nor regret followed my passionate outburst. I had not loved the doll. In the still, dark world in which I lived there was no strong **sentiment** or tenderness. I felt my teacher sweep the fragments to one side of the hearth, and I had a sense of satisfaction that the cause of my discomfort was removed. She brought me my hat, and I knew I was going out into the warm sunshine. This thought, if a wordless sensation may be called a thought, made me hop and skip with pleasure.

7　We walked down the path to the well-house, attracted by the fragrance of the honeysuckle with which it was covered. Some one was drawing water and my teacher placed my hand under the spout. As the cool stream gushed over one hand she spelled into the other the word water, first slowly, then rapidly. I stood still, my whole attention fixed upon the motions of her fingers. Suddenly I felt a misty consciousness as of something forgotten--a thrill of returning thought; and somehow the mystery of language was **revealed** to me. I knew then that "w-a-t-e-r" meant the wonderful cool something that was flowing over my hand. That living word awakened my soul, gave it light, hope, joy, set it free! There were barriers still, it is true, but barriers that could in time be swept away.

8 I left the well-house eager to learn. Everything had a name, and each name gave birth to a new thought. As we returned to the house every object which I touched seemed to quiver with life. That was because I saw everything with the strange, new sight that had come to me. On entering the door I remembered the doll I had broken. I felt my way to the hearth and picked up the pieces. I tried vainly to put them together. Then my eyes filled with tears; for I realized what I had done, and for the first time I felt repentance and sorrow.

9 I learned a great many new words that day. I do not remember what they all were; but I do know that mother, father, sister, teacher were among them— words that were to make the world blossom for me, "like Aaron's rod, with flowers." It would have been difficult to find a happier child than I was as I lay in my crib at the close of that eventful day and lived over the joys it had brought me, and for the first time longed for a new day to come.

✏ WRITE

PERSONAL RESPONSE: When Keller realizes that the "finger play" in her palm actually signifies the water she's feeling, she experiences an epiphany: everything has a name. Think about an important discovery you made as a child. Perhaps you learned the correct meaning of a word you misunderstood or found out that a growling dog may bite. In a personal response, compare and contrast your experience with Keller's and draw conclusions about how learning can affect children.

Please note that excerpts and passages in the StudySync® library and this workbook are intended as touchstones to generate interest in an author's work. The excerpts and passages do not substitute for the reading of entire texts, and StudySync® strongly recommends that students seek out and purchase the whole literary or informational work in order to experience it as the author intended. Links to online resellers are available in our digital library. In addition, complete works may be ordered through an authorized reseller by filling out and returning to StudySync® the order form enclosed in this workbook.

Reading & Writing Companion **83**

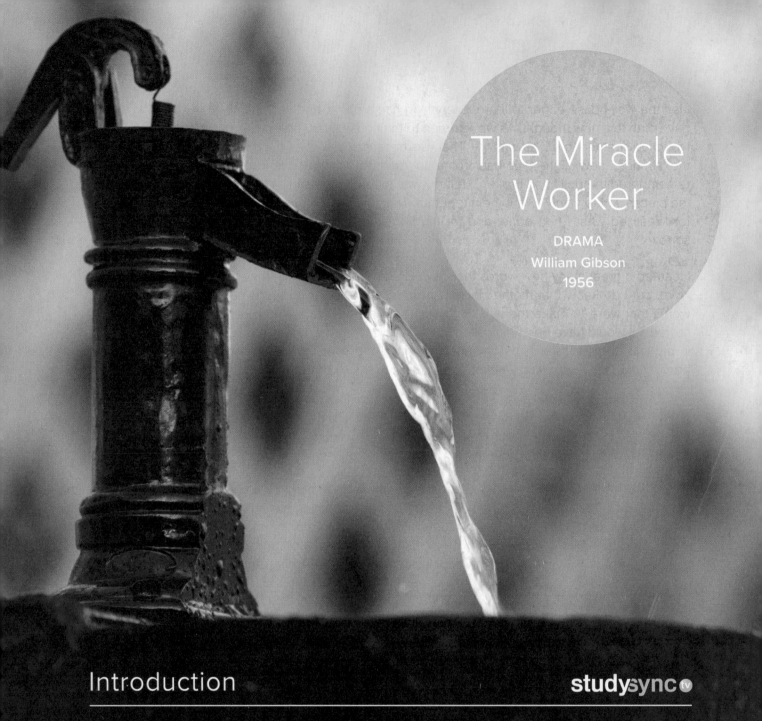

The Miracle Worker

DRAMA
William Gibson
1956

Introduction

studysync TV

*T*he *Miracle Worker* by William Gibson (1914–2008) was not only an award-winning Broadway play, but also an Academy Award-winning film. Based on the autobiography of Helen Keller, *The Story of My Life, The Miracle Worker* presents an emotional account of Keller's early life, after an illness caused her to lose her sight and hearing. The excerpt here comes from Act III of the play, and illustrates the unflagging efforts of teacher Annie Sullivan to break through Helen's walls of darkness and silence. In sharing the story of Helen Keller, who went on to become a world-famous author and political activist, Gibson provides a powerful portrait of two strong-willed females guided by the spirit of determination.

"She's testing you. You realize?"

NOTES

CHARACTERS:

ANNIE SULLIVAN: young teacher trained to work with the blind and deaf; in her early twenties
HELEN KELLER: child who has been blind and deaf since infancy; now seven years old
KATE KELLER: Helen's mother; in her early thirties
CAPTAIN KELLER: Helen's father; middle-aged
JAMES KELLER: Captain Keller's grown son by a previous marriage; in his early twenties
AUNT EV: Captain Keller's sister; middle-aged
VINEY: Keller family servant

TIME: The 1880s
PLACE: In and around the Keller homestead in Tuscumbia, Alabama

1　[Now in the family room the rear door opens, and HELEN steps in. She stands a moment, then sniffs in one deep grateful breath, and her hands go out **vigorously** to familiar things, over the door panels, and to the chairs around the table, and over the silverware on the table, until she meets VINEY; she pats her flank approvingly.]

2　VINEY: Oh, we glad to have you back too, prob'ly.

3　[HELEN hurries groping to the front door, opens and closes it, removes its key, opens and closes it again to be sure it is unlocked, gropes back to the rear door and repeats the procedure, removing its key and hugging herself gleefully. AUNT EV is next in by the rear door, with a relish tray; she bends to kiss HELEN'S cheek. HELEN finds KATE behind her, and thrusts the keys at her.]

4　KATE: What? Oh.

5　[To EV]

6　Keys.

Skill: Dramatic Elements and Structure

The setting gives useful information. I can imagine how the characters looked in 1880's Alabama and how the room is set up. I can get a good sense of Helen from the stage directions, even though she can't say anything. She's grateful to be home and she knows the location of all the familiar things in the house. She touches them.

7   [She pockets them, lets HELEN feel them.]

8   Yes, I'll keep the keys. I think we've had enough of locked doors, too.

9   [JAMES, having earlier put ANNIE'S suitcase inside her door upstairs and taken himself out of view around the corner, now reappears and comes down the stairs as ANNIE and KELLER mount the porch steps. Following them into the family room, he pats ANNIE'S hair in passing, rather to her surprise.]

10   JAMES: Evening, general.

11   [He takes his own chair opposite. VINEY bears the empty water pitcher out to the porch. The remaining suggestion of garden house is gone now, and the water pump is unobstructed; VINEY pumps water into the pitcher. KATE surveying the table breaks the silence.]

12   KATE: Will you say grace, Jimmie?

13   [They bow their heads, except for HELEN, who palms her empty plate and then reaches to be sure her mother is there. JAMES considers a moment, glances across at ANNIE, lowers his head again, and obliges.]

14   JAMES [Lightly]: And Jacob was left alone, and wrestled with an angel until the breaking of the day; and the hollow of Jacob's thigh was out of joint, as he wrestled with him; and the angel said, Let me go, for the day breaketh. And Jacob said, I will not let thee go, except thou bless me. Amen.

15   [ANNIE has lifted her eyes suspiciously at JAMES, who winks expressionlessly and **inclines** his head to HELEN.]

16   Oh, you angel.

17   [The others lift their faces; VINEY returns with the pitcher, setting it down near KATE, then goes out the rear door; and ANNIE puts a napkin around HELEN.]

18   AUNT EV: That's a very strange grace, James.

19   KELLER: Will you start the muffins, Ev?

20   JAMES: It's from the Good Book, isn't it?

21   AUNT EV [Passing a plate]: Well, of course it is. Didn't you know?

22   JAMES: Yes, I knew.

23   KELLER [Serving]: Ham, Miss Annie?

24 ANNIE: Please.

25 AUNT EV: Then why ask?

26 JAMES: I meant it is from the Good Book, and therefore a fitting grace.

27 AUNT EV: Well, I don't know about that.

28 KATE [With the pitcher]:Miss Annie?

29 ANNIE: Thank you.

30 AUNT EV: There's an awful lot of things in the Good Book that I wouldn't care to hear just before eating.

31 [When ANNIE reaches for the pitcher, HELEN removes her napkin and drops it to the floor. ANNIE is filling HELEN'S glass when she notices it; she considers HELEN'S bland expression a moment, then bends, **retrieves** it, and tucks it around HELEN'S neck again.]

32 JAMES: Well, fitting in the sense that Jacob's thigh was out of joint, and so is this piggie's.

33 AUNT EV: I declare, James—

34 KATE: Pickles, Aunt Ev?

35 AUNT EV: Oh, I should say so, you know my opinion of your pickles—

36 KATE: This is the end of them, I'm afraid. I didn't put up nearly enough last summer, this year I intend to— [She interrupts herself, seeing HELEN **deliberately** lift off her napkin and drop it again to the floor. She bends to retrieve it, but ANNIE stops her arm.]

37 KELLER [Not noticing]: Reverend looked in at the office today to complain his hens have stopped laying. Poor fellow, he was out of joint, all he could— [He stops too, to frown down the table at KATE, HELEN, and ANNIE in turn, all suspended in mid-motion.]

38 JAMES [Not noticing]: I've always suspected those hens.

39 AUNT EV: Of what?

40 JAMES: I think they're Papist. Has he tried— [He stops, too, following KELLER'S eyes. ANNIE now stops to pick the napkin up.]

Please note that excerpts and passages in the StudySync® library and this workbook are intended as touchstones to generate interest in an author's work. The excerpts and passages do not substitute for the reading of entire texts, and StudySync® strongly recommends that students seek out and purchase the whole literary or informational work in order to experience it as the author intended. Links to online resellers are available in our digital library. In addition, complete works may be ordered through an authorized reseller by filling out and returning to StudySync® the order form enclosed in this workbook.

Reading & Writing Companion

87

NOTES

41 AUNT EV: James, now you're pulling my—lower extremity, the first thing you know we'll be—

42 [She stops, too, hearing herself in the silence. ANNIE, with everyone now watching, for the third time puts the napkin on HELEN. HELEN yanks it off, and throws it down. ANNIE rises, lifts HELEN'S plate, and bears it away. HELEN, feeling it gone, slides down and commences to kick up under the table; the dishes jump. ANNIE **contemplates** this for a moment, then coming back takes HELEN'S wrists firmly and swings her off the chair. HELEN struggling gets one hand free, and catches at her mother's skirt; when KATE takes her by the shoulders, HELEN hangs quiet.]

43 KATE: Miss Annie.

44 ANNIE: No.

45 KATE [A pause]: It's a very special day.

46 ANNIE [Grimly]: It will be, when I give in to that.

47 [She tries to disengage HELEN'S hand; KATE lays hers on ANNIE'S.]

48 ANNIE: Captain Keller.

49 KELLER [Embarrassed]: Oh, Katie, we—had a little talk, Miss Annie feels that if we indulge Helen in these—

50 AUNT EV: But what's the child done?

51 ANNIE: She's learned not to throw things on the floor and kick. It took us the best part of two weeks and—

52 AUNT EV: But only a napkin, it's not as if it were breakable!

53 ANNIE: And everything she's learned is? Mrs. Keller, I don't think we should—play tug-of-war for her, either give her to me or you keep her from kicking.

54 KATE: What do you wish to do?

55 ANNIE: Let me take her from the table.

56 AUNT EV: Oh, let her stay, my goodness, she's only a child, she doesn't have to wear a napkin if she doesn't want to her first evening—

57 ANNIE [Level]: And ask outsiders not to interfere.

Skill: Dramatic Elements and Structure

Annie and Aunt Ev's disagreement tells me about their characters. Annie thinks Helen should have consequences when she breaks the rules, but Aunt Ev doesn't want to punish her. She thinks that Helen should be able to do what she wants. I wonder if this will be part of the main conflict of the plot.

58 AUNT EV [Astonished]: Out—outsi—I'm the child's aunt!

59 KATE [Distressed]: Will once hurt so much, Miss Annie? I've—made all Helen's favorite foods, tonight.

60 [A pause.]

61 KELLER [Gently]: It's a homecoming party, Miss Annie.

62 [ANNIE after a moment releases HELEN. But she cannot accept it, at her own chair she shakes her head and turns back, intent on KATE.]

63 ANNIE: She's testing you. You realize?

64 JAMES [To ANNIE]: She's testing you.

65 KELLER: Jimmie, be quiet.

66 [JAMES sits, tense.]

67 Now she's home, naturally she—

68 ANNIE: And wants to see what will happen. At your hands. I said it was my main worry, is this what you promised me not half an hour ago?

69 KELLER [Reasonably]: But she's not kicking, now—

70 ANNIE: And not learning not to. Mrs. Keller, teaching her is **bound** to be painful, to everyone. I know it hurts to watch, but she'll live up to just what you demand of her, and no more.

71 JAMES [Palely]: She's testing you.

72 KELLER [Testily]: Jimmie.

73 JAMES: I have an opinion, I think I should—

74 KELLER: No one's interested in hearing your opinion.

75 ANNIE: I'm interested, of course she's testing me. Let me keep her to what she's learned and she'll go on learning from me. Take her out of my hands and it all comes apart.

Excerpted from *The Miracle Worker* by William Gibson, published by Simon & Schuster.

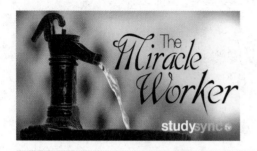

First Read

Read "The Miracle Worker." After you read, complete the Think Questions below.

☁ THINK QUESTIONS

1. Who is Annie Sullivan, and why is she at the Keller homestead in Tuscumbia, Alabama? Cite evidence from information and ideas that are directly stated and from ideas you have inferred from clues in the text.

2. How would you describe Annie's emotions? Why is she feeling this way? Cite evidence from the text to support your answer.

3. What do you think Annie means when she says, "Take her out of my hands and it all comes apart"? Cite evidence from the text to support your answer.

4. Use context clues to determine the meaning of **retrieves** as it is used in line 31. Write your definition of *retrieves* and explain how you figured out its meaning.

5. Read the following dictionary entry:

bound \bound\
noun

1. a limitation or restriction
2. a leap or jump

verb

1. to walk in leaping or jumping strides

adjective

1. certain or likely to do something

Which definition most closely matches the meaning of **bound** as it is used in line 70? Write the appropriate definition of *bound* here and explain how you figured out the correct meaning.

Skill: Dramatic Elements and Structure

Use the Checklist to analyze Dramatic Elements and Structure in "The Miracle Worker." Refer to the sample student annotations about Dramatic Elements and Structure in the text.

••• CHECKLIST FOR DRAMATIC ELEMENTS AND STRUCTURE

In order to identify key dramatic elements, note the following:

- ✓ stage directions, including descriptions of

  - the design of the stage
  - the movement of characters
  - sounds or music

- ✓ the main characters and other characters

- ✓ the dialogue between the characters

Analyze how the playwright develops characters through dialogue and staging, using the following questions as a guide:

- ✓ What do the characters say to each other through dialogue?

- ✓ What does the dialogue reveal about the characters and the plot?

- ✓ What do I learn about the characters and the plot by reading the stage directions?

Please note that excerpts and passages in the StudySync® library and this workbook are intended as touchstones to generate interest in an author's work. The excerpts and passages do not substitute for the reading of entire texts, and StudySync® strongly recommends that students seek out and purchase the whole literary or informational work in order to experience it as the author intended. Links to online resellers are available in our digital library. In addition, complete works may be ordered through an authorized reseller by filling out and returning to StudySync® the order form enclosed in this workbook.

Reading & Writing
Companion

91

Skill: Dramatic Elements and Structure

Reread paragraphs 68–75 from "The Miracle Worker." Then, using the Checklist on the previous page, answer the multiple-choice questions below.

⟳ YOUR TURN

1. What does the dialogue between Captain Keller and Annie in lines 68–70 tell the reader about the drama's theme?

   ○ A. Annie is interested in having Captain Keller discontinue his service.

   ○ B. Annie is going to continue to fight to help Helen learn, even if it's hard.

   ○ C. Annie is afraid that Helen will lose the will to learn as time passes.

   ○ D. Annie is irritated that James is not willing to do what it takes for Helen to learn.

2. What does the stage direction in line 72 reveal about Captain Keller's attitude toward his son James?

   ○ A. Captain Keller values James's opinions.

   ○ B. Captain Keller thinks James is being too hard on Annie.

   ○ C. Captain Keller does not value James's opinions.

   ○ D. Captain Keller encourages James to speak during family meetings.

3. In what way is Annie's dialogue in line 75 likely to affect the plot?

   ○ A. It is likely Helen will be taken from the table.

   ○ B. It is likely Helen will be allowed to stay at the table.

   ○ C. It is likely Annie will resign her teaching post.

   ○ D. It is likely Annie and James will begin to date.

Close Read

Reread "The Miracle Worker." As you reread, complete the Skills Focus questions below. Then use your answers and annotations from the questions to help you complete the Write activity.

◎ SKILLS FOCUS

1. One of the purposes of stage directions is to describe the actions of the characters. Highlight evidence in the stage directions for *The Miracle Worker* that helps you understand the conflicts among various characters. Explain how the evidence helps you understand the conflict conflict that drives the plot.

2. Identify evidence in the dialogue of conflict between the characters in *The Miracle Worker*. Explain what the dialogue reveals about the plot.

3. One of the themes in *The Miracle Worker* is the ability of a teacher to transform a student's life. Identify evidence in the drama that develops this theme and explain your reasoning.

4. Highlight examples of dialogue where Helen is discussed. What do the characters' words reveal about what they want for Helen?

5. In Chapter IV of *The Story of My Life,* Helen Keller tells the story of meeting Annie Sullivan, the teacher who changed her life. Langston Hughes tells Helen's story of overcoming her physical challenges in his poem "Helen Keller." Identify evidence that helps you determine what story William Gibson tells in *The Miracle Worker.* Explain what the story is.

✎ WRITE

COMPARATIVE: What is the conflict of the play and how is it resolved? Compare the conflict and resolution of the conflict in the play with those that are presented in "Helen Keller" by Langston Hughes and Keller's autobiography, *The Story of My Life.* Cite specific scenes or dialogue that contribute to the play's conflict and resolution to support your response.

Extended
Oral
Project

EXTENDED
ORAL
PROJECT

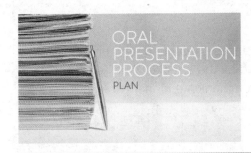

Oral Presentation Process: Plan

PLAN	DRAFT	REVISE	EDIT AND PRESENT

Stories are powerful. It's easy to get lost in a great fiction story like "Damon and Pythias," or a true account, like that of Melba Pattillo Beals in *Warriors Don't Cry*. All stories, including those from the *Making Your Mark* unit, have the ability to influence your perspective, or how you see the world. Your own stories are powerful, too. Maybe you've lived through something that shaped one of your core beliefs. Is there an event in your life that contributed to a strong opinion you hold? What is it?

WRITING PROMPT

What is something you believe in?

Think about something for which you hold a position or take a stance. How did you come to adopt this position? What experience, event, person, or story shaped your belief? Give an organized presentation with a specific stance and position. Tell a story from your life that explains how you adopted your position. Your story should focus on a singular moment or experience from your life and clearly relate to your position or stance. As you prepare your presentation, consider the following:

- A position or stance is a belief or opinion that you hold.

- A story that supports your position should have a clear beginning, middle, and end.

- Your presentation should be about yourself.

In your presentation, be sure to employ the following in order to communicate your ideas effectively:

- a specific stance and position

- eye contact

- speaking rate

- volume

- enunciation

- natural gestures

- media components or visual displays

- conventions of language

Introduction to Oral Presentation

Argumentative oral presentations that are based on personal experiences use anecdotes, or short stories about people and events, to support a specific position or stance held by the speaker. They are organized in a classic story structure and use effective speaking techniques to communicate ideas. The characteristics of this type of argumentative oral presentation include:

- a specific position or stance

- anecdotes, or stories, that support the position or stance

- a classic story structure with a beginning, middle, and end

- consistent eye contact and natural gestures

- clear oral communication

- integration of multimedia and visual displays

- a works cited page

As you continue with this Extended Oral Project, you'll receive more instruction and practice at crafting each of the characteristics of argumentative writing to create your own oral presentation.

Before you get started on your own argumentative oral presentation, read this oral presentation that one student, Lorenzo, wrote in response to the writing prompt. As you read the Model, highlight and annotate the features of argumentative writing that Lorenzo included in his oral presentation.

STUDENT MODEL

Dress for Success

Introduction:

I choose to wear comfortable clothes. Some people scoff at my jorts (jean shorts), but these faded beauties are as soft as a blanket. Others have questioned my sock choices. But it makes no difference to me whether one sock is green and ankle-length and the other is knee-high and ornamented with Halloween pumpkins. My t-shirt is two sizes too large for the tallest kid in school, and definitely too big for me.

DRESS FOR SUCCESS

AUTHOR: LORENZO

Claim:

But I find both utility and pride in the clothing I wear. I believe that your clothes should make it possible for you to do the thing you love the most.

CLOTHING SHOULD...

- Create pride in the wearer
- Be useful and beneficial to the wearer
- Make it possible to do what you love

NOTES

Narrative Context:

The thing I love the most is drumming. You may not be familiar with just how physically intense drumming can be, but some drummers really go wild when they play.

What I wear when I play is important—hence my unstylish uniform; but I didn't always know that.

Narrative Beginning:

Last year, I was going for a spot at the prestigious Summer Music Academy. SMA is a music camp. However, this camp is neither crafts nor kayaking. This camp is ten hours a day of musical boot camp, where young hopefuls like myself learn to hone their technique from the best teachers. Some of whom are even famous!

I drum daily. So, I was pumped to audition. Let me revise that statement, I was both pumped and terrified! Still, I knew that if I drummed my heart out, I would be fine. I might even get in.

SUMMER MUSIC ACADEMY INFO

- Musical boot camp for young musicians admitted through audition only
- Ten hours of instrumental practice and theory per day
- World famous teachers

Narrative Middle:

Ariana, who is my older sister, is the smartest and coolest person I know. I look up to her, and I know she cares about me. So, when she took me shopping for my audition and outfitted me in a suit, I tried to quiet the voice in my head that said: *this ridiculous suit isn't you.*

And so, at the suggestion (more like demand) of my sister Ariana (who gets scary when she makes demands), I wore a tight, uncomfortable suit to the biggest audition of my life.

Please note that excerpts and passages in the StudySync® library and this workbook are intended as touchstones to generate interest in an author's work. The excerpts and passages do not substitute for the reading of entire texts, and StudySync® strongly recommends that students seek out and purchase the whole literary or informational work in order to experience it as the author intended. Links to online resellers are available in our digital library. In addition, complete works may be ordered through an authorized reseller by filling out and returning to StudySync® the order form enclosed in this workbook.

Reading & Writing Companion

99

Narrative Climax:

I walked into my audition with my head held high (because my collar was so stiff) and my arms calmly at my sides (because I could barely move them). I sat down behind the drum set, picked up my sticks, and created a beat.

Well, I tried to. When I wanted to tappa-tappa-tappa-kish, I tappa-tappa-tappa-missed. The sounds I produced had neither beat nor rhythm. My arms were stuck so tightly in my sleeves that I kept missing the surface of the drum. It was like *Titanic, Part 2*. I went full speed ahead and—bam—I ran right into the iceberg.

I failed, and the judges unanimously agreed.

Narrative Falling Action:

I slunk out of the audition room, totally embarrassed. I felt that I had made a fool of myself. As I waited for my ride, this girl sat down next to me. She was carrying an instrument in a big case. She said, "Hey, I'm Jules. Sorry it didn't work out in there."

I shook my head. I was too upset to talk.

Jules said, "You know, I bombed my first big performance because I insisted on wearing these crazy, white, studded high heels during my solo. Right in the middle of everything, I not only fell over but also knocked three other saxophonists out of their chairs!" She laughed at herself. "It's not about what you wear, it's about how you play."

GEMS OF ADVICE FROM JULES

- "I bombed my first big performance because I insisted on wearing these crazy white, studded high heels during my solo."
- "It's not about what you wear, it's about how you play."

Narrative Falling Action Detail:

I looked at Jules, who was dressed plainly in jeans and flannel. She had braces and messy long brown hair, but there was something about her that was truly cool. I thought about the drummers I had seen in photos and videos. Like Jules, they were truly cool and wore clothes that made drumming easy.

Narrative End:

That night when I got home, I took off my suit and immediately put back on my uniform of jorts and t-shirt. I set up my selfie stick and turned my phone on video mode. I pressed record and played the set I intended to play earlier. I moved like electricity. More importantly, I felt like myself.

That night I sent the SMA my video, hoping the judges might recognize my skills and passion for drumming. A week later, the message I had been waiting for arrived in my inbox.

BE TRUE TO YOURSELF

- I put on my jorts and felt like myself.
- The judges saw the real me in my video: a passionate, skilled drummer.

Conclusion:

According to scientists at Northwestern University, ". . . new research shows that wearing certain items of clothing identified with certain qualities could help improve performance…" (McGregor). Whether it's a three-piece suit or a pair of jorts and a too-big t-shirt, wear the clothes that help you do the things you love. My name is Lorenzo and I am a proud, jorts-wearing student at the Summer Music Academy.

WORKS CITED

McGregor, Jena. "New study: What you wear could affect how well you work." *The Washington Post.* 10 Mar. 2012. www.washingtonpost.com/blogs/post-leadership/post/new-study-what-you-wear-could-affect-how-well-you-work/2011/04/01/gIQAssHomR_blog.html

Works Cited

McGregor, Jena. "New study: What you wear could affect how well you work." *The Washington Post*, 10 Mar. 2012, www.washingtonpost.com/blogs/post-leadership/post/new-study-what-you-wear-could-affect-how-well-you-work/2011/04/01/gIQAssHomR_blog.html

Please note that excerpts and passages in the StudySync® library and this workbook are intended as touchstones to generate interest in an author's work. The excerpts and passages do not substitute for the reading of entire texts, and StudySync® strongly recommends that students seek out and purchase the whole literary or informational work in order to experience it as the author intended. Links to online resellers are available in our digital library. In addition, complete works may be ordered through an authorized reseller by filling out and returning to StudySync® the order form enclosed in this workbook.

Reading & Writing Companion **103**

WRITE

Writers often take notes about ideas before they sit down to prepare their presentation. Think about what you've learned so far about oral presentations and organizing argumentative writing to help you begin prewriting.

- **Purpose:** What are some things that you believe in?

- **Audience:** What message do you want your audience to take away from your presentation?

- **Position/Claim:** Which of these could you tell a story about to illustrate your position?

- **Relevant Evidence/Anecdote:** What happened to help you adopt this position? What challenge or conflict did you have to deal with? Did you learn something or change in some way?

- **Engaging the Audience/Oral Presentation Skills:** How do you want to tell your story? Will you be humorous, serious, inspirational? How can you use technology and visuals to engage your audience?

Response Instructions

Use the questions in the bulleted list to write a one-paragraph summary. Your summary should describe what will happen in your argumentative oral presentation.

Don't worry about including all of the details now; focus only on the most essential and important elements. You will refer back to this short summary as you continue through the steps of the writing process.

Skill: Evaluating Sources

••• CHECKLIST FOR EVALUATING SOURCES

First, reread the sources you gathered and identify the following:

- what kind of source it is, including video, audio, or text, and where the source comes from
- where information seems inaccurate, biased, or outdated
- where information seems irrelevant or incomplete

In order to use advanced searches to gather relevant, credible, and accurate print and digital sources, use the following questions as a guide:

- Is the source material written by a recognized expert on the topic?
- Is the source material published by a well-respected author or organization?
- Is the material up-to-date or based on the most current information?
- Is the material factual, and can it be verified by another source?
- Is the source material connected to persons or organizations that are objective and unbiased?
- Does the source contain omissions of important information?

YOUR TURN

Read the factors below. Then, complete the chart by sorting them into those that show that a source is credible and reliable and those that do not.

Factors	
A	The text is based on the opinions of one person.
B	The author is a reporter for an internationally recognized newspaper.
C	The article is from the 1950s.
D	The text is informational and includes research from a well-recognized university.
E	The website is for a personal podcast.
F	The article includes clear arguments based on facts.

Credible and Reliable	Not Credible or Reliable

⟳ YOUR TURN

Complete the chart by filling in the title and author of a source you are considering using for your own oral presentation and answering the questions about it.

Question	My Source
Source Title and Author: Are the title and author clearly identified?	
Reliability: Is the material up-to-date or based on the most current information?	
Credibility: Is the source material written by a recognized expert on the topic? Is the source material published by a well-respected author or organization?	
Accuracy: Is the material factual, and can it be verified by another source?	

Please note that excerpts and passages in the StudySync® library and this workbook are intended as touchstones to generate interest in an author's work. The excerpts and passages do not substitute for the reading of entire texts, and StudySync® strongly recommends that students seek out and purchase the whole literary or informational work in order to experience it as the author intended. Links to online resellers are available in our digital library. In addition, complete works may be ordered through an authorized reseller by filling out and returning to StudySync® the order form enclosed in this workbook.

Reading & Writing Companion **107**

Skill: Organizing an Oral Presentation

••• CHECKLIST FOR ORGANIZING AN ORAL PRESENTATION

In order to present claims and findings using appropriate eye contact, adequate volume, and clear pronunciation, do the following:

- decide whether your presentation will be delivered to entertain, critique, inform, or persuade

- identify your audience in order to create your content

- choose a style for your oral presentation, either formal or informal

- present claims and any information you have found, sequencing your ideas and information logically

- make sure your descriptions, facts, and details accentuate and support the main idea of your presentation

- include multimedia components such as graphics, images, music or sound effects, and visual displays in your presentation to clarify information

- use appropriate eye contact, adequate volume, and clear pronunciation

To present claims and findings using appropriate eye contact, adequate volume, and clear pronunciation, consider the following questions:

- Have I decided on the purpose of my presentation and identified my audience?

- Have I put my facts and ideas in a logical sequence?

- Did I make sure the descriptions, facts, and details accentuate and support the main idea of my presentation?

- Do my facts and details accentuate and support the main idea?

- Did I include multimedia components to clarify information?

- Have I practiced using appropriate eye contact, adequate volume, and clear pronunciation?

↻ YOUR TURN

Read each idea below. Then, complete the chart by matching each idea with its correct place in the presentation sequence.

Ideas	
A	I kept clipping a little more here and there, trying to even up the poor dog's coat.
B	Believe me, there is nothing cute about a bald golden retriever.
C	Never assume that anyone can do something just because the process looks easy.
D	photo of a golden retriever
E	Unfortunately for my dog, you can't glue hair back on.
F	Now I know that there are some things an amateur shouldn't tackle—like clipping a dog.
G	I woke up one morning and thought, "How hard could it be to clip my golden retriever?"

Presentation Sequence	Idea
Hook	
Position	
Story beginning	
Story middle	
Story end	
How experience shaped position	
Media or visual component	

YOUR TURN

Complete the chart below by writing a short summary of your ideas for each section of your presentation.

Outline	Summary
Hook	
Position	
Story beginning	
Story middle	
Story end	
How experience shaped position	
Media or visual component	

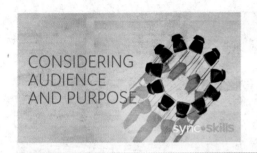

Skill: Considering Audience and Purpose

••• CHECKLIST FOR CONSIDERING AUDIENCE AND PURPOSE

In order to present claims and findings using appropriate eye contact, adequate volume, and clear pronunciation, note the following:

- when writing your presentation, sequence your ideas, facts, or explanations in a logical order, such as the order in which events occurred

- use pertinent, or valid, and important facts and details to support and accentuate, or highlight, the main ideas or themes in your presentation

- use appropriate eye contact

- speak at an adequate volume, so you can be heard by everyone

- use correct pronunciation

- remember to adapt, or change, your speech according to your task, and if it is appropriate, use formal English and not language you would use in ordinary conversation

To better understand how to present claims and findings and use appropriate eye contact, adequate volume, and clear pronunciation, consider the following questions:

- Have I used appropriate eye contact when giving my presentation?

- Did I speak at an adequate volume and use correct pronunciation?

- Did I sequence ideas in a logical order, such as the order in which events occurred?

- Have I used valid and important facts and details? Have I accentuated, or highlighted, these details?

- If necessary, have I used formal English in my presentation?

Please note that excerpts and passages in the StudySync® library and this workbook are intended as touchstones to generate interest in an author's work. The excerpts and passages do not substitute for the reading of entire texts, and StudySync® strongly recommends that students seek out and purchase the whole literary or informational work in order to experience it as the author intended. Links to online resellers are available in our digital library. In addition, complete works may be ordered through an authorized reseller by filling out and returning to StudySync® the order form enclosed in this workbook.

Reading & Writing Companion   111

YOUR TURN

Read the excerpts from Nik and Dakota's presentation on characters below. Then, complete the chart by identifying whether the register is formal or informal.

Excerpts	
A	Because he's a troublemaker!
B	And the way characters are designed is called characterization.
C	And, like with all those characters, their traits are revealed through their own words, thoughts, and actions.
D	Like Elmer Fudd for Bugs Bunny.
E	I know! There are so many good ones!
F	The main character is called the protagonist.

Formal	Informal

✏ WRITE

Take turns reading your presentation aloud to a partner. When you finish, write a reflection about how well your register, vocabulary, tone, and voice suited your audience and purpose. What aspects did you apply well? What aspects did you struggle with? How can you improve in the future?

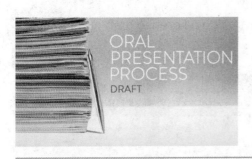

Oral Presentation Process: Draft

PLAN	DRAFT	REVISE	EDIT AND PRESENT

You have already made progress toward writing your oral presentation. Now it is time to draft your oral presentation.

✏ WRITE

Use your plan and other responses in your Binder to draft your oral presentation. You may also have new ideas as you begin drafting. Feel free to explore those new ideas as you have them. You can also ask yourself these questions:

- Have I taken a specific position or stance?

- Have I included anecdotes, or stories, that support my position or stance?

- Have I employed a classic story structure with a clear beginning, middle, and end?

Before you submit your draft, read it over carefully. You want to be sure you've responded to all aspects of the prompt.

Please note that excerpts and passages in the StudySync® library and this workbook are intended as touchstones to generate interest in an author's work. The excerpts and passages do not substitute for the reading of entire texts, and StudySync® strongly recommends that students seek out and purchase the whole literary or informational work in order to experience it as the author intended. Links to online resellers are available in our digital library. In addition, complete works may be ordered through an authorized reseller by filling out and returning to StudySync® the order form enclosed in this workbook.

Reading & Writing Companion 113

Here is Lorenzo's oral presentation draft. As you read, identify details that help Lorenzo grab his audience's attention and understand his position.

NOTES

Skill:
Communicating
Ideas

Lorenzo revises sentences to add information or to clarify meaning for the audience.

STUDENT MODEL: FIRST DRAFT

Dress for Success

~~I choose to wear comfortable clothes. Some people scoff at my jorts, but these faded beauties are as soft as a blanket.~~ I choose to wear comfortable clothes. Some people scoff at my jorts (jean shorts), but these faded beauties are as soft as a blanket. Others have questioned my sock choices. But it makes no difference to me whether one sock is green and ankle-length and the other is knee-high and ornamented with Halloween pumpkins. My t-shirt is two sizes too large for the tallest kid in school, and definitely too big for me. But I find both utility and pride in the clothing I wear. I believe that your clothes should make it possible for you to do the thing you love the most.

The thing I love the most is drumming. You may not be familiar with just how physically intense drumming can be, but some drummers really go wild when they play.

What I wear when I play is important. This explains my unstylish uniform.

I was going for a spot at the prestigious Summer Music Academy. SMA is a music camp. However, this camp is neither crafts or kayaking. This camp is ten hours a day of musical boot camp, where young hopefuls like me learn to hone their technique from the best teachers. Some of who are even famous!

I drum daily, so, I was pumped to audition, let me revise that statement, I was like woah man! Still, I knew that if I drummed my heart out, I would be fine. I might even get in.

Ariana, who is my older sister, is not only the scariest and smartest and coolest person I know. I look up to her, and I know she cares about me. So, when she took me shopping for my audition and outfitted me in a suit, I tried to quiet the voice in my head that said: *this rediculous suit isn't you.*

And so, at the suggestion (more like demand) of my sister Ariana (who gets scary when she makes demands), I wore a tight, uncomfortable suit to the biggest audition of my life.

I walked into my audition with my head held high and my arms calmly at my sides. I sat down behind the drum set, picked up my sticks, and created a beat.

Please note that excerpts and passages in the StudySync® library and this workbook are intended as touchstones to generate interest in an author's work. The excerpts and passages do not substitute for the reading of entire texts, and StudySync® strongly recommends that students seek out and purchase the whole literary or informational work in order to experience it as the author intended. Links to online resellers are available in our digital library. In addition, complete works may be ordered through an authorized reseller by filling out and returning to StudySync® the order form enclosed in this workbook.

Reading & Writing Companion 115

Well, I tried to. The sounds I produced had neither beat nor rhythm. My arms were stuck so tightly in my sleeves that I kept missing the surface of the drum. It was like *Titanic, Part 2*. I went full speed ahead and—bam—I ran right into the iceberg.

I failed, and the judges unanimusly agreed.

I walked out of the audition room, totally embarrassed. I felt that I had made a fool of myself. As I waited for my ride, this girl sat down next to me. She was carrying an instrument in a big case. She said, "Hey, I'm Jules. Sorry it didn't work out in there."

I shook my head. I was too upset to talk.

Jules said, "You know, I bombed my first big performance because I insisted on wearing these crazy, white, studded high heels during my solo. Right in the middle of everything, I fell over but also knocked three other saxophonists out of their chairs!" She laughed at her. "It's not about what you wear, it's about how you play."

I looked at Jules, which was dressed plainly in jeans and flannel. She had braces and messy long brown hair, but there was something about her that was so totally awesome dude. I thought about the drummers I had seen in photos and videos. Like Jules, they were truly cool and wore clothes that made drumming easy.

~~That night when I got home, I took off my suit. I immediately put back on my uniform of jorts and t-shirt. I set up my selfie stick. Then I turned my phone on video mode. I pressed record and played the set I intended to play earlier. I moved like electricity, and I felt like me.~~

That night when I got home, I took off my suit and immediately put back on my uniform of jorts and t-shirt. I set up my selfie stick and turned my phone on video mode. I pressed record and played the set I intended to play earlier. I moved like electricity. More importantly, I felt like myself.

That night I sent the SMA my video. I hoped the judges might recognize my skills. I hoped they would recognize passion for drumming. A week later I found out. The message I had been waiting for arrived in my inbox.

Scientists at Northwestern University, have done studies that prove that the clothes we wear affect how we think and what we feel. Our clothes give us confidence. Whether it's a three-piece suit or a pair of jorts and a too-big t-shirt, wear the clothes that help you do the things you love. My name is Lorenzo and I am a proud, jorts-wearing student at the Summer Music Academy.

Works Cited

McGregor, Jena. "New study: What you wear could affect how well you work." *The Washington Post*, 10 Mar. 2012, www.washingtonpost.com/blogs/post-leadership/post/new-study-what-you-wear-could-affect-how-well-you-work/2011/04/01/gIQAssHomR_blog.html

Skill: Reasons and Relevant Evidence

Lorenzo wants to include evidence to explain how comfy clothes helped him achieve his goal. He examines his argumentative oral presentation—he clearly states his claim, and he adds reasons and relevant evidence to support his position.

Skill: Sources and Citations

Lorenzo realizes that he should have a Works Cited list. He makes sure to include the author, title, publisher, publication day, and the web address. By including all the required information, Lorenzo gives proper credit to the sources he used. It also lets readers find these sources on their own.

Skill: Communicating Ideas

In order to present claims and findings using appropriate eye contact, adequate volume, and clear pronunciation, note the following:

- when writing your presentation, sequence your ideas, facts, or explanations in a logical order, such as the order in which events occurred

- use pertinent, or valid, and important facts and details to support and accentuate, or highlight, the main ideas or themes in your presentation

- remember to use appropriate eye contact

- speak at an adequate volume, so you can be heard by everyone

- use correct pronunciation

To better understand how to present claims and findings and use appropriate eye contact, adequate volume, and clear pronunciation, consider the following questions:

- Have I used appropriate eye contact when giving my presentation?

- Did I speak at an adequate volume and use correct pronunciation?

- Did I sequence ideas in a logical order, such as the order in which events occurred?

- Have I used valid and important facts and details? Have I accentuated these details?

YOUR TURN

Read the examples of students using different presentation strategies to communicate their ideas. Then, complete the chart by identifying the correct strategy to match each example.

Strategies	
A	make eye contact
B	use gestures
C	pay attention to posture
D	speak clearly

Example	Strategy
A student moves her arm in a quick downward motion when talking about a tree crashing to the ground.	
A student slows his rate of speech and clearly enunciates his position.	
A student looks directly at one audience member and then another while speaking.	
A student stands front and center with her shoulders squared.	

WRITE

Take turns reading your presentation aloud to a partner.

When you are presenting:

- Employ steady eye contact to help keep your listeners' attention.

- Use appropriate speaking rate, volume, and enunciation to clearly communicate with your listeners.

- Use natural gestures to add meaning and interest as you speak.

- Keep in mind conventions of language, and avoid informal or slang speech.

When you finish, write a reflection about your experience of using presentation strategies to effectively communicate your ideas. Which strategies did you implement well? Which strategies did you struggle with? Which strategies did you find most helpful? How can you improve in the future?

Skill: Reasons and Relevant Evidence

••• CHECKLIST FOR REASONS AND RELEVANT EVIDENCE

As you begin to determine what reasons and relevant evidence will support your claim(s), use the following questions as a guide:

- What is the claim (or claims) that I am making in my argument?

- Are the reasons I have included clear and easy to understand?

- What relevant evidence am I using to support this claim?

- Have I selected evidence from credible sources, and are they relevant to my claim?

- Am I quoting the source evidence accurately?

Use the following steps as a guide to help you determine how you will support your claim(s) with clear reasons and relevant evidence, using credible sources:

- identify the claim(s) you will make in your argument

- establish clear reasons for making your claim(s)

- select evidence from credible sources that will convince others to accept your claim(s)

  > look for reliable and relevant sources of information online, such as government or educational websites

  > search print resources such as books written by an expert or authority on a topic

- explain the connection between your claim(s) and the evidence selected

Please note that excerpts and passages in the StudySync® library and this workbook are intended as touchstones to generate interest in an author's work. The excerpts and passages do not substitute for the reading of entire texts, and StudySync® strongly recommends that students seek out and purchase the whole literary or informational work in order to experience it as the author intended. Links to online resellers are available in our digital library. In addition, complete works may be ordered through an authorized reseller by filling out and returning to StudySync® the order form enclosed in this workbook.

Reading & Writing Companion **121**

YOUR TURN

Choose the best answer for each question.

1. Which sentence, added to the end of the paragraph in the box, would best support Lorenzo's claim?

> Jules said, "You know, I bombed my first big performance because I insisted on wearing these crazy, white, studded high heels during my solo. Right in the middle of everything, I fell over but also knocked three other saxophonists out of their chairs!" She laughed at herself.

- ○ A. "Man, I was uncomfortable!"
- ○ B. "It's not about what you wear, it's about how you play."
- ○ C. "I was so upset."
- ○ D. "So, wear whatever you want, whenever you want to!"

2. Which reason should Lorenzo add to clarify the end of his oral presentation, in the box below?

> My name is Lorenzo and I am a proud, jorts-wearing student at the Summer Music Academy.

- ○ A. So, in conclusion, wear what you like.
- ○ B. You can wear a three-piece suit or a too-big t-shirt.
- ○ C. I'm so happy my dream came true—Summer Music Academy is the place for me!
- ○ D. Whether it's a three-piece suit or a pair of jorts and an oversized t-shirt, wear the clothes that help you do the things you love.

 WRITE

Use the questions in the checklist to revise your oral presentation.

Skill:
Sources and Citations

••• CHECKLIST FOR SOURCES AND CITATIONS

In order to cite and gather sources of information, do the following:

- select and gather information from a variety of print and digital sources relevant to a topic

- check that sources are credible, or reliable and trustworthy, and avoid relying on or overusing one source

- be sure that facts, details, and other information support the central idea or claim and demonstrate your understanding of the topic or text

- use parenthetical citations or footnotes or endnotes to credit sources

- include all sources in a bibliography, following a standard format:

  > Halall, Ahmed. *The Pyramids of Ancient Egypt*. New York: Central Publishing, 2016.

  > for a citation or footnote, include the author, title, and page number

To check that sources are gathered and cited correctly, consider the following questions:

- Did I give credit to sources for all of my information to avoid plagiarism?

- Have I relied on one source, instead of looking for different points of view on my topic in other sources?

- Did I include all my sources in my bibliography?

- Are my citations formatted correctly using a standard, accepted format?

Please note that excerpts and passages in the StudySync® library and this workbook are intended as touchstones to generate interest in an author's work. The excerpts and passages do not substitute for the reading of entire texts, and StudySync® strongly recommends that students seek out and purchase the whole literary or informational work in order to experience it as the author intended. Links to online resellers are available in our digital library. In addition, complete works may be ordered through an authorized reseller by filling out and returning to StudySync® the order form enclosed in this workbook.

Reading & Writing Companion

123

YOUR TURN

Choose the best answer to each question.

1. Lorenzo did not reference any print sources in his presentation; however, if he had found a book on drumming that included a chapter on what drummers should wear, what information should he have included at the end of a sentence referencing this material?

   ○ A. Add the author's last name in parentheses after the quotation.

   ○ B. Add the page number in parentheses after the quotation.

   ○ C. Add the author's last name and the page number in parentheses after the quotation.

   ○ D. He wouldn't need a citation.

2. Below is a citation for another article that Lorenzo found but did not use in his presentation. What information is he missing?

   Hutson, Matthew and Tori Rodriguez. "Dress for Success: How Clothes Influence Our Performance." *Scientific American*. www.scientificamerican.com/article/dress-for-success-how-clothes-influence-our-performance/

   ○ A. None. All the information is there.

   ○ B. The title of the article is missing.

   ○ C. The name(s) of the author(s) is missing.

   ○ D. The date of publication is missing.

 WRITE

Use the questions in the checklist to write and revise your Works Cited list. Refer to the *MLA Handbook* as needed.

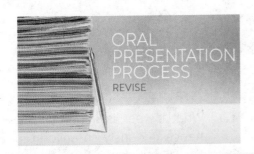

Oral Presentation Process: Revise

PLAN	DRAFT	REVISE	EDIT AND PRESENT

You have written a draft of your oral presentation. You have also received input from your peers about how to improve it. Now you are going to revise your draft.

⏴ REVISION GUIDE

Examine your draft to find areas for revision. Keep in mind your purpose and audience as you revise for clarity, development, organization, and style. Use the guide below to help you review:

Review	Revise	Example
Clarity		
Highlight any places in your presentation where your position or ideas are unclear because of a lack of information or vague wording.	Revise sentences to add information or to clarify meaning for the audience.	I choose to wear comfortable clothes. Some people scoff at my jorts (jean shorts), but these faded beauties are as soft as a blanket.
Development		
Identify places where you can add interesting details or use humor to make your point and keep your audience engaged.	Insert descriptive details or use hyperbole or other forms of humor to enliven your discussion.	Still, I walked into my audition with my head held high (because my collar was so stiff) and my arms calmly at my sides (because I could barely move them). I sat down behind the drum set, picked up my sticks, and created a beat.

Review	Revise	Example
Organization		
Annotate the places in your presentation where you begin your story or transition from the beginning to the middle or from the middle to the end.	Add a transition that makes it clear that you are beginning your story or moving from the beginning to the middle or from the middle to the end.	• What I wear is important—hence my unstylish uniform. But I didn't always know that. • Last year, I was going for a spot at the prestigious Summer Music Academy. SMA is a music camp.
Style: Word Choice		
Identify simple action verbs.	Select sentences to rewrite using more expressive action verbs.	I ~~walked~~ slunk out of the audition room, totally embarrassed.
Style: Sentence Variety		
Look for strings of sentences that have similar lengths. Annotate any place where a conjunction or transition could vary the length of the sentences you use.	Use conjunctions to join together short, choppy sentences or separate long sentence by adding a transition.	That night when I got home, I took off my ~~suit. I~~ suit and immediately put back on my uniform of jorts and t-shirt. I set up my ~~selfie stick. Then I~~ selfie stick and turned my phone on video mode. I pressed record and played the set I intended to play earlier. I moved like ~~electricity, and~~ electricity. More importantly, I felt like myself.

✏ **WRITE**

Use the guide above, as well as your peer reviews, to help you evaluate your oral presentation to determine areas that should be revised.

Oral Presentation Process: Edit and Present

PLAN	DRAFT	REVISE	EDIT AND PRESENT

You have revised your argumentative oral presentation based on your peer feedback and your own examination.

Now, it is time to edit your oral presentation. When you revised, you focused on the content of your presentation. You probably looked at the clarity of your position and argument, the development of your story structure, and whether your word choices and anecdotes were engaging and supportive of your position. When you edit, you focus on the mechanics of your oral presentation, paying close attention to things like grammar and punctuation.

Use the checklist below to guide you as you edit:

☐ Have I ensured that all pronouns are in the correct form?

☐ Have I varied my sentence patterns for meaning and listener interest?

☐ Have I maintained a consistent style and tone?

☐ Do I have any sentence fragments or run-on sentences?

☐ Have I spelled everything correctly?

Notice some edits Lorenzo has made:

- Created sentence variety by changing three short, choppy sentences into one longer, more varied sentence.

- Changed the incorrect usage of *or* to *nor*.

- Changed an incorrect intensive pronoun.

- Maintained consistency in style by changing slang dialogue to more descriptive words.

~~What I wear when I play is important. This explains my unstylish uniform.~~ What I wear when I play is important—hence my unstylish uniform. But I didn't always know that.

Last year, I was going for a spot at the prestigious Summer Music Academy. SMA is a music camp. However, this camp is neither crafts ~~or~~ nor kayaking. This camp is ten hours a day of musical boot camp, where young hopefuls like ~~me~~ myself learn to hone their technique from the best teachers. Some of who are even famous!

I drum daily. So, I was pumped to audition. Let me revise that statement, ~~I was like woah man!~~ I was both pumped and terrified! Still, I knew that if I drummed my heart out, I would be fine. I might even get in.

✏ WRITE

Use the questions above, as well as your peer reviews, to help you evaluate your argumentative oral presentation to determine areas that need editing. Then edit your oral presentation to correct those errors.

Once you have made all your corrections, you are ready to present your work. You may present it to your class or to a group of your peers. You can record your presentation to share with family and friends, or to post on your blog. If you publish online, share the link with your family, friends, and classmates.

Stage Sets Through History

INFORMATIONAL TEXT

Introduction

How has the experience of viewing a play changed over time? Even when the dialogue is the same as it was hundreds of years ago, the look of the play is different, thanks to the scenery that surrounds it.

VOCABULARY

transported

carried away to

symmetrical

describing something with two halves that are identical

derives

originates from

aligned

to agree with or be in the correct or matching position

perspective

drawing something in two dimensions to add length, height, and depth

NOTES

READ

1　Suppose you go to a Broadway musical. The curtain rises. You see the dramatic scenery. You may be **transported** to a jungle. You may find yourself on a 1960s city block. The stage set, or scenery, tells you when and where the action will take place.

2　Theater has entertained people for nearly 3,000 years. It took a long time for stage sets to become an important part of that entertainment.

EARLY STAGES

3　In the time of the ancient Greeks, heroes and villains performed on a bare stage.

Amphitheater at Acropolis, Athens

4   The first scenery was a small tent on the stage. Actors changed their clothes there. The tent was called a *skene*. The word *scenery* **derives** from that word.

5   Sophocles wrote plays in ancient Greece. He may have been the first person to use painted scenery. A painted cloth hung on the skene. It showed a place or set a mood. We call such a painting a *backdrop*.

ADDING SCENERY

6   In 1600s Italy, scenery became a key part of plays. Two inventions led to this change. One was the understanding of **perspective** in art. In stage sets, perspective could make things look far away. The other invention was a new kind of stage. This type of stage had a proscenium arch, which helped to frame the performers. The architect Giovanni Battista Aleotti perfected this design in 1618. It is still used today.

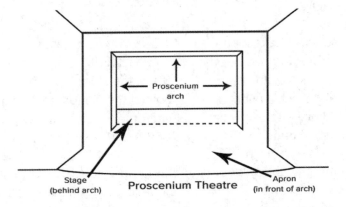

Proscenium Theatre

Proscenium arch

Stage (behind arch)

Apron (in front of arch)

7   During the 1600s, stage sets were grand, but they were not realistic. Aleotti painted scenes on canvas. These scenes lined the back of the stage. They were fancy and **symmetrical**. The same set stayed up for the whole play.

REALISTIC SETTINGS

8   The 1800s saw big changes in stage sets. Plays became more realistic, and the setting was now very important. Designers made the stage look like a boxed room. They used furniture and props that matched the set. The set fit the historical period of the play. A so-called "box set" might even have a ceiling. The whole set fit onto the stage. The idea was that the audience formed the invisible "fourth wall" of the set. Audience members felt as though they were peering into a real home. They could watch the action from their seats behind the fourth wall.

9   Today, set designs are sometimes realistic. Sometimes, though, they have just a few objects on the stage. The objects give hints to the setting. A ladder might stand in for a fire escape. A piano on the apron might indicate a jazz club. A bale of hay or a painted silo might let an audience imagine the calves and chickens on a farm in Oklahoma.

THEN AND NOW

10   Suppose you saw Shakespeare's *The Merry Wives of Windsor* in the 1600s. The stage set would have been a painted backdrop. It might show the town of Windsor. If you saw the play in the 1800s, the stage set would change for every scene and act. It might show a room at the Garter Inn. It might change to show Windsor Park. Each canvas backdrop would look as real as possible. Each would be **aligned** to the time when the play takes place.

11   If you saw the play today, you might see a bare set. The set might use the apron as well as the stage. It might include just tiny hints about the scenery. A sign might tell you that you are in the Garter Inn. A tree in a pot might stand for Windsor Park. The play has not changed, but the use of stage sets has changed a great deal.

First Read

Read the story. After you read, answer the Think Questions below.

☁ THINK QUESTIONS

1. What is the main topic of the text?

   _____

   _____

2. What information does this text give?

   _____

   _____

3. What is one way plays and stage sets have changed in the present day?

   _____

   _____

4. Use context to confirm the meaning of the word *aligned* as it is used in "Stage Sets Through History." Write your definition of *aligned* here.

   _____

   _____

5. What is another way to say that the word "scenery" *derives* from the word "skene"?

   _____

   _____

Please note that excerpts and passages in the StudySync® library and this workbook are intended as touchstones to generate interest in an author's work. The excerpts and passages do not substitute for the reading of entire texts, and StudySync® strongly recommends that students seek out and purchase the whole literary or informational work in order to experience it as the author intended. Links to online resellers are available in our digital library. In addition, complete works may be ordered through an authorized reseller by filling out and returning to StudySync® the order form enclosed in this workbook.

Reading & Writing Companion 133

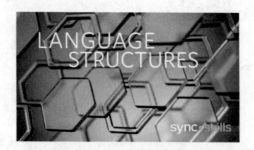

Skill:
Language Structures

★ DEFINE

In every language, there are rules that tell how to **structure** sentences. These rules define the correct order of words. In the English language, for example, a **basic** structure for sentences is subject, verb, and object. Some sentences have more **complicated** structures.

You will encounter both basic and complicated **language structures** in the classroom materials you read. Being familiar with language structures will help you better understand the text.

••• CHECKLIST FOR LANGUAGE STRUCTURES

To improve your comprehension of language structures, do the following:

 Monitor your understanding.

- Ask yourself: Why do I not understand this sentence? Is it because I do not understand some of the words? Or is it because I do not understand the way the words are ordered in the sentence?

- Pay attention to coordinating conjunctions.

  > **Coordinating conjunctions** are used to join words or groups of words that have equal grammatical importance.

  > The coordinating conjunction *and* shows that two or more things are true of a person, object, or event.

    Example: Josefina is a good athlete **and** student.

  > The coordinating conjunction *or* shows a choice between different possibilities.

    Example: Josefina can either do her homework **or** go for a run.

  > The coordinating conjunction *but* shows a contrast between people, objects, or events.

    Example: Josefina wants to run **but** should finish her homework first.

- Break down the sentence into its parts.

  > Ask yourself: What ideas are expressed in this sentence? Are there conjunctions that join ideas or show contrast?

✓ Confirm your understanding with a peer or teacher.

YOUR TURN

Read the sentence from the text. Write the letter of the correct function of the underlined conjunction in the sentence.

Function	
A	connecting choices
B	connecting contrasting ideas
C	connecting similar or related ideas
D	connecting similar or related words

Sentence	Function
They used furniture <u>and</u> props that matched the set.	
Plays became more realistic, <u>and</u> the setting was now very important.	
A bale of hay <u>or</u> a painted silo might let an audience imagine the calves and chickens on a farm in Oklahoma.	
During the 1600s, stage sets were grand, <u>but</u> they were not realistic.	

Skill:
Visual and Contextual Support

★ DEFINE

Visual support is an image or an object that helps you understand a text. **Contextual support** is a **feature** that helps you understand a text. By using visual and contextual supports, you can develop your vocabulary so you can better understand a variety of texts.

First, preview the text to identify any visual supports. These might include illustrations, graphics, charts, or other objects in a text. Then, identify any contextual supports. Examples of contextual supports are titles, heads, captions, and boldface terms. Write down your **observations**.

Then, write down what those visual and contextual supports tell you about the meaning of the text. Note any new vocabulary that you see in those supports. Ask your peers and your teacher to **confirm** your understanding of the text.

••• CHECKLIST FOR VISUAL AND CONTEXTUAL SUPPORT

To use visual and contextual support to understand texts, do the following:

- ✓ Preview the text. Read the title, headers, and other features. Look at any images and graphics.

- ✓ Write down the visual and contextual supports in the text.

- ✓ Write down what those supports tell you about the text.

- ✓ Note any new vocabulary that you see in those supports.

- ✓ Create an illustration for the reading and write a descriptive caption.

- ✓ Confirm your observations with your peers and teacher.

YOUR TURN

Read the following excerpt from the text. Then, complete the multiple-choice questions below.

---

from "Stage Sets Through History"

ADDING SCENERY

In 1600s Italy, scenery became a key part of plays. Two inventions led to this change. One was the understanding of perspective in art. In stage sets, perspective could make things look far away. The other invention was a new kind of stage. This type of stage had a proscenium arch, which helped to frame the performers. The architect Giovanni Battista Aleotti perfected this design in 1618. It is still used today.

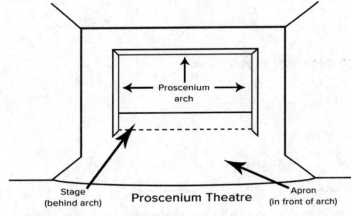

---

1. The heading tells you that in the period of history described in this section

   ○ A. people did not yet use scenery in plays
   ○ B. plot was more important than scenery
   ○ C. scenery became a part of stage sets
   ○ D. actors had to build their own scenery

2. According to the diagram, the "new kind of stage" was known as a(n)

   ○ A. apron
   ○ B. proscenium
   ○ C. arch
   ○ D. stage

STAGE SETS
THROUGH
HISTORY

Close Read

✏ WRITE

INFORMATIONAL: Choose one section of "Stage Sets Through History" to summarize in a short report, begin with a topic sentence. Then tell the main ideas and details of the section in your own words. Pay attention to the spelling of plural nouns as you write.

Use the checklist below to guide you as you write.

☐ Which section did you choose to summarize?

☐ What was the topic of that section?

☐ What are some key ideas you learned from that section?

Use the sentence frames to organize and write your informational paragraph.

In the section of text called "_____,"

the author tells about _____.

At the time being discussed, _____

_____.

For example, _____

_____.

One feature of scenery in these times might have been _____

_____.

Six Too Many

DRAMA

Introduction

I n Nonno's Italian childhood, the holidays featured a special feast. His grandchildren are used to more modern traditions. Lydia is willing to be open-minded, but Ben is miserable as the meal begins. Can his grandfather win him over?

 VOCABULARY

distinctive

having a characteristic that makes a person or thing different from others

vigil

a period of watching and waiting, as in preparation for a holy day

delectable

highly delicious or pleasing

tureen

a deep, covered serving dish

succession

a series of things or events; one following another; sequence

 NOTES

☰ READ

1 [*SCENE 1: A modern-day dining room. MOTHER, BEN, and LYDIA are seated at a long table with a holiday centerpiece and candles. A Christmas tree is visible through an archway.*]

2 MOTHER (*turning to her children*): Now, remember, kids—we are skipping the usual turkey and stuffing. Nonno asked to share something **distinctive** from his childhood.

3 BEN (*sulking*): We know, Mom. The Feast of the Seven Dumb Fishes. Like fish are what people eat on Christmas Eve!

4 LYDIA: Well, I like fish—some kinds, anyway. And it's Nonno's house.

5 BEN (*crossly*): I could see one fish, maybe, as an appetizer. But seven? That's at least six too many.

6   MOTHER: Shh. Here comes Nonno with the first course!

7   [*NONNO (Grandfather) enters proudly, bearing a platter.*]

8   MOTHER (*helping to serve*): Tell us about the dish, Papa! Salt cod, **delectable**! (BEN *groans.*)

9   NONNO: Well, it's not everyone's cup of tea, but it is traditional to start the meal this way. We'll be having a **succession** of small plates, like that tapas restaurant that is Lydia's favorite. Just a few bites until the final dish.... (BEN *groans again.*)

10   LYDIA: Ignore Ben, Nonno. He's been driving us up the wall complaining about traditions.

11   NONNO (*winking*): Well, there are traditions and traditions, you know. My family's Christmas Eve tradition is probably just a bit older than yours, Ben! We have served this kind of food for generations.

12   MOTHER: Originally, the idea was that we Italians were waiting for Christmas, holding a kind of **vigil**, and eating meat was not allowed.

13   NONNO: That's right, and just as we always had eaten fish on Fridays, we ate fish on Christmas Eve. (*He sits, takes his fork, and starts to eat the salt cod. BLACKOUT.*)

14   [*SCENE 2: Later, that same evening. The family is still at the table, which is littered with dishes. NONNO enters, bearing a* **tureen**.]

15   LYDIA (*groaning*): Oh, Nonno, I honestly don't think I could eat another bite! Those clams were wonderful, but the gross little octopus bodies on skewers nearly killed me!

16   NONNO: Nonsense! I spent all day making this from scratch; it's Ben's favorite! (*He lifts the lid, and steam rises.*)

17   BEN (*amazed*): Nonno! You made a cioppino? We haven't had fish stew since Nonna died! I actually forgot it existed!

18   NONNO: Your grandmother would never forgive me if I didn't include a cioppino. I remember when you were small, you would call her on the phone and tell her to make it for you the next time you visited.

19   BEN: It was such an important part of our trips to see you! I would help Nonna in the kitchen, and she always called on you to chop the heads off the fish.

20 MOTHER (*a bit tearfully*): I'm surprised you remember, Ben—you were so little!

21 LYDIA: I barely remember, but that glorious smell is reminding me!

22 NONNO (*serving the stew into bowls*): This, in a nutshell, is why we take our ancestors' traditions and pass them down. Smelling this wonderful stew reminds me of your grandmother, but it also reminds me of my own grandmother in Salerno. One day, perhaps, Ben or Lydia will make the Feast of the Seven Fishes for their children, and the smells and tastes will take them back to today.

23 BEN (*rising to help* NONNO *hand around the bowls*): We will come early next year so you can show me how to make cioppino. I definitely will need you to chop off the heads, though. (MOTHER *and* LYDIA *look at each other in surprise, shrug, and laugh.*)

24 LYDIA: What happened to "six too many"?

25 BEN (*shrugging*): Seven was just right. Although I must say salt cod is not my favorite.

26 NONNO (*raising his glass*): To traditions! (*The others toast and drink.* CURTAIN.)

SIX TOO MANY

First Read

Read the story. After you read, answer the Think Questions below.

1. Who are the main characters in the play? What is their relationship?

   _____

   _____

2. Where and when do the two scenes in the play take place?

   _____

   _____

3. At the end of the play, who changes his or her mind? Explain.

   _____

   _____

4. Use context to confirm the meaning of the word *succession* as it is used in "Six Too Many." Write your definition of *succession* here.

   _____

   _____

5. What is another way to say that a meal is *distinctive*?

   _____

   _____

Please note that excerpts and passages in the StudySync® library and this workbook are intended as touchstones to generate interest in an author's work. The excerpts and passages do not substitute for the reading of entire texts, and StudySync® strongly recommends that students seek out and purchase the whole literary or informational work in order to experience it as the author intended. Links to online resellers are available in our digital library. In addition, complete works may be ordered through an authorized reseller by filling out and returning to StudySync® the order form enclosed in this workbook.

Reading & Writing Companion **143**

Skill: Analyzing Expressions

★ DEFINE

When you read, you may find English expressions that you do not know. An **expression** is a group of words that communicates an idea. Three types of expressions are idioms, sayings, and figurative language. They can be difficult to understand because the meanings of the words are different from their **literal**, or usual, meanings.

An **idiom** is an expression that is commonly known among a group of people. For example, "It's raining cats and dogs" means it is raining heavily. **Sayings** are short expressions that contain advice or wisdom. For instance, "Don't count your chickens before they hatch" means do not plan on something good happening before it happens. Figurative language is when you describe something by comparing it with something else, either directly (using the words *like* or *as*) or indirectly. For example, "I'm as hungry as a horse" means I'm very hungry. None of the expressions are about actual animals.

••• CHECKLIST FOR ANALYZING EXPRESSIONS

To determine the meaning of an expression, remember the following:

✓ If you find a confusing group of words, it may be an expression. The meaning of words in expressions may not be their literal meaning.

- Ask yourself: Is this confusing because the words are new? Or because the words do not make sense together?

✓ Determining the overall meaning may require that you use one or more of the following:

- context clues

- a dictionary or other resource

- teacher or peer support

✓ Highlight important information before and after the expression to look for clues.

⟳ YOUR TURN

Read the following excerpt from the text. Then, complete the multiple-choice questions below.

---

from "Six Too Many"

LYDIA [*groaning*]: Oh, Nonno, I honestly don't think I could eat another bite! Those clams were wonderful, but the gross little octopus bodies on skewers nearly killed me!

NONNO: Nonsense! I spent all day making this from scratch; it's Ben's favorite! [*He lifts the lid, and steam rises.*]

---

1. When Lydia says the octopus "nearly killed" her, she means that

    ○ A. she choked on the skewers
    ○ B. octopi can be dangerous
    ○ C. she prefers clams
    ○ D. the dish was too much for her

2. The context clue that best supports this is:

    ○ A. "Oh, Nonno"
    ○ B. "don't think I could eat another bite"
    ○ C. "clams were wonderful"
    ○ D. "on skewers"

3. Which word or words from Nonno's speech are an expression?

    ○ A. Nonsense
    ○ B. all day
    ○ C. from scratch
    ○ D. Ben's favorite

4. What does Nonno's expression probably mean?

    ○ A. "from start to finish"
    ○ B. "with itchy components"
    ○ C. "with a pointed object"
    ○ D. "scraped together with fingernails"

Skill:
Analyzing and Evaluating Text

★ DEFINE

Analyzing and **evaluating** a text means reading carefully to understand the author's **purpose** and **message**. In informational texts, authors may provide information or opinions on a topic. They may be writing to inform or persuade a reader. In fictional texts, the author may be **communicating** a message or lesson through their story. They may write to entertain or to teach the reader something about life.

Sometimes authors are clear about their message and purpose. When the message or purpose is not stated directly, readers will need to look closer at the text. Readers can use textual evidence to make inferences about what the author is trying to communicate. By analyzing and evaluating the text, you can form your own thoughts and opinions about what you read.

••• CHECKLIST FOR ANALYZING AND EVALUATING TEXT

In order to analyze and evaluate a text, do the following:

✓ Look for details that show why the author is writing.

- Ask yourself: Is the author trying to inform, persuade, or entertain? What are the main ideas of this text?

✓ Look for details that show what the author is trying to say.

- Ask yourself: What is the author's opinion about this topic? Is there a lesson I can learn from this story?

✓ Form your own thoughts and opinions about the text.

- Ask yourself: Do I agree with the author? Does this message apply to my life?

YOUR TURN

Student Instructions: Read the following excerpt from the text. Then, complete the multiple choice questions below.

---

from "Six Too Many"

NONNO (*serving the stew into bowls*): This, in a nutshell, is why we take our ancestors' traditions and pass them down. Smelling this wonderful stew reminds me of your grandmother, but it also reminds me of my own grandmother in Salerno. One day, perhaps, Ben or Lydia will make the Feast of the Seven Fishes for their children, and the smells and tastes will take them back to today.

---

1. Nonno hopes to persuade his grandchildren to

   ○ A. eat the stew he has made
   ○ B. reflect on their past
   ○ C. remember their grandmother
   ○ D. pass on a nice tradition

2. What happens to Nonno when he smells the fish stew?

   ○ A. He pretends that he is at home in Italy.
   ○ B. He realizes how much he loves his grandchildren.
   ○ C. He recalls important people from his past.
   ○ D. He imagines a future time with Lydia and Ben.

3. What does the author probably believe about traditions?

   ○ A. They should change with the times.
   ○ B. They are important to protect and to pass on.
   ○ C. They are mostly meaningful to older people.
   ○ D. They have little to do with modern life.

4. What is Nonno's lesson for Ben?

   ○ A. Family traditions can connect the present to the past.
   ○ B. Grandparents are a valuable part of your life.
   ○ C. Not everyone is lucky enough to have a grand feast.
   ○ D. A life of service is a good and happy life.

Please note that excerpts and passages in the StudySync® library and this workbook are intended as touchstones to generate interest in an author's work. The excerpts and passages do not substitute for the reading of entire texts, and StudySync® strongly recommends that students seek out and purchase the whole literary or informational work in order to experience it as the author intended. Links to online resellers are available in our digital library. In addition, complete works may be ordered through an authorized reseller by filling out and returning to StudySync® the order form enclosed in this workbook.

Reading & Writing Companion   **147**

SIX TOO MANY

Close Read

✏️ **WRITE**

PERSONAL NARRATIVE: In "Six Too Many," Ben changes his mind about some traditions. Think of a tradition that your family has. It may have to do with holidays, or it may be completely unrelated. Describe the tradition using specific details, and tell your feelings about it. Give reasons for your feelings. Have they changed over time? Pay attention to main and helping verbs as you write.

Use the checklist below to guide you as you write.

☐ What is one tradition that your family has?

☐ How did you feel about this tradition in the past? Why?

☐ How do you feel about this tradition now? Why?

Use the sentence frames to organize and write your personal narrative.

One tradition my family has is _____

_____.

We always _____

_____.

When I was younger, I felt _____

_____.

More recently, I feel _____

_____.

 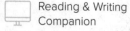

PHOTO/IMAGE CREDITS:

cover, iStock.com/danibeder
Melba Pattillo Beals - 615 collection / Alamy Stock Photo
Langston Hughes - Underwood Archives / Contributor/ Archive Photos/ Getty Images
William Gibson - Colin McPherson / Contributor/ Corbis Entertainment/ Getty Images
Shirley Jackson - Bloomberg / Contributor/ Bloomberg/ Getty Images
Helen Keller - Time Life Pictures / Contributor/ The LIFE Picture Collection
Piri Thomas - Chris Felver / Contributor/ Premium Archive/ Getty Images
p. 4, Public Domain
p. 5, iStock.com/Caval
p. 6, iStock.com/Caval
p. 7, iStock.com/Murat Göçmen
p. 8, iStock.com/Murat Göçmen
p. 9, Public Domain
p. 10, ©iStock.com/tolgabayraktar
p. 18, ©iStock.com/tolgabayraktar
p. 19, iStock.com/Gemini-Create
p. 20, iStock.com/Gemini-Create
p. 22, iStock.com/GreenPimp
p. 23, iStock.com/GreenPimp
p. 24, ©iStock.com/tolgabayraktar
p. 25, iStock.com/Viktor_Gladkov
p. 30, iStock.com/wdstock
p. 36, iStock.com/Viktor_Gladkov
p. 37, iStock.com/deimagine
p. 38, iStock.com/deimagine
p. 39, iStock.com/Viktor_Gladkov
p. 40, iStock.com/Chaturong
p. 45, iStock.com/Chaturong
p. 46, iStock.com/antoni_halim
p. 47, iStock.com/antoni_halim
p. 48, iStock.com/Chaturong
p. 49, goodmoments
p. 56, goodmoments
p. 57, iStock.com/yipengge
p. 58, iStock.com/yipengge
p. 59, goodmoments
p. 60, iStock.com/CaroleGomez
p. 63, iStock.com/bagi1998
p. 67, iStock.com/SaladinoSA
p. 73, iStock.com/bagi1998
p. 74, iStock.com/Max_Xie
p. 75, iStock.com/Max_Xie
p. 76, iStock.com/bagi1998
p. 77, iStock.com/ANRiPhoto
p. 80, iStock.com/FSTOPLIGHT
p. 81, Corbis Historical/Getty Images

p. 84, melissasanger/iStock.com
p. 90, melissasanger/iStock.com
p. 91, iStock/Spanishalex
p. 92, iStock/Spanishalex
p. 93, melissasanger/iStock.com
p. 94, iStock.com/hanibaram, iStock.com/seb_ra, iStock.com/Martin Barraud
p. 94, iStock.com/Martin Barraud
p. 95, iStock.com/Martin Barraud
p. 97, FPO
p. 97, FPO
p. 98, FPO
p. 98, FPO
p. 99, FPO
p. 99, FPO
p. 100, FPO
p. 100, FPO
p. 101, FPO
p. 101, FPO
p. 103, iStock.com/Mutlu Kurtbas
p. 106, iStock.com/BilevichOlga
p. 109, iStock.com/Martin Barraud
p. 111, iStock.com/Martin Barraud
p. 112, iStock.com/PhotoBylove
p. 113, iStock.com/carloscastilla
p. 114, NBC Universal Archives
p. 116, iStock.com/polesnoy
p. 119, iStock.com/Domin_domin
p. 121, iStock.com/tofumax
p. 123, iStock.com/Martin Barraud
p. 125, iStock.com/Martin Barraud
p. 127, iStock.com/nito100
p. 128, iStock.com/PeopleImages
p. 128, iStock.com/monkeybusinessimages
p. 128, iStock.com/Wavebreakmedia
p. 128, iStock.com/PrinPrince
p. 128, iStock.com/DanielPrudek
p. 129, iStock.com/Richmatts
p. 130, iStock.com
p. 131, iStock.com/nito100
p. 132, iStock.com/BlackJack3D
p. 134, iStock.com/AlexandrBognat
p. 136, iStock.com/nito100
p. 137, iStock.com/MichellePatrickPhotographyLLC
p. 138, iStock.com/sgcallaway1994
p. 138, iStock.com/SrdjanPav
p. 138, iStock.com/TkKurikawa
p. 138, iStock.com/ThamKC
p. 138, iStock.com/lvdprod
p. 141, iStock.com/MichellePatrickPhotographyLLC
p. 142, iStock.com/Ales_Utovko
p. 144, iStock.com/kyoshino
p. 146, iStock.com/MichellePatrickPhotographyLLC

Please note that excerpts and passages in the StudySync® library and this workbook are intended as touchstones to generate interest in an author's work. The excerpts and passages do not substitute for the reading of entire texts, and StudySync® strongly recommends that students seek out and purchase the whole literary or informational work in order to experience it as the author intended. Links to online resellers are available in our digital library. In addition, complete works may be ordered through an authorized reseller by filling out and returning to StudySync® the order form enclosed in this workbook.

Reading & Writing Companion

149

studysync®

Text Fulfillment Through StudySync

If you are interested in specific titles, please fill out the form below and we will check availability through our partners.

ORDER DETAILS

Date:

TITLE	AUTHOR	Paperback/ Hardcover	Specific Edition *If Applicable*	Quantity

SHIPPING INFORMATION

Contact:

Title:

School/District:

Address Line 1:

Address Line 2:

Zip or Postal Code:

Phone:

Mobile:

Email:

BILLING INFORMATION   ☐ *SAME AS SHIPPING*

Contact:

Title:

School/District:

Address Line 1:

Address Line 2:

Zip or Postal Code:

Phone:

Mobile:

Email:

PAYMENT INFORMATION

☐ CREDIT CARD   Name on Card:

Card Number: Expiration Date: Security Code:

☐ PO   Purchase Order Number:

StudySync Text Fulfillment, BookheadEd Learning, LLC
610 Daniel Young Drive | Sonoma, CA 95476